Prentice-Hall
Contemporary Topics in Accounting Series

ALFRED RAPPAPORT, SERIES EDITOR

BEDFORD, *Extensions in Accounting Disclosure*

DYCKMAN, DOWNES, AND MAGEE, *Efficient Capital Markets and Accounting: A Critical Analysis*

JAEDICKE AND SPROUSE, *Accounting Flows: Income, Funds, and Cash*

KELLER AND PETERSON, *The Uniformity-Flexibility Issue in Accounting*

LEV, *Financial Statement Analysis: A New Approach*

PALMER, *Analytical Foundations of Planning, Programming, Budgeting Systems*

REVSINE, *Replacement Cost Accounting*

SHANK, *Accounting for Intercorporate Investments*

WAGNER, *Auditing and the Computer*

ZEFF AND SEIDLER, *A Critical Analysis of the Accounting Principles Board*

EFFICIENT
CAPITAL MARKETS
AND ACCOUNTING
A CRITICAL ANALYSIS

THOMAS R. DYCKMAN
Cornell University

DAVID H. DOWNES
University of California at Berkeley

ROBERT P. MAGEE
University of Chicago

PRENTICE-HALL, INC., ENGLEWOOD CLIFFS, NEW JERSEY

Library of Congress Cataloging in Publication Data

DYCKMAN, THOMAS R.
    Efficient capital markets and accounting.

    (Prentice-Hall contemporary topics in accounting
series)
    Bibliography: p.
    Includes index.
    1. Corporations—United States—Finance. 2. Corporations—
United States—Accounting. 3. Financial statements—
United States. I. Downes, David H., joint author.
II. Magee, Robert P., joint author. III. Title.
HG4063.D9   658.1′52   75-9716
ISBN 0-13-246975-8
ISBN 0-13-246967-7 pbk.

PRINTED IN THE UNITED STATES OF AMERICA

10 9 8 7 6 5 4 3 2 1

Prentice-Hall International, Inc., LONDON
Prentice-Hall of Australia, Pty. Ltd., SYDNEY
Prentice-Hall of Canada, Ltd., TORONTO
Prentice-Hall of India Private Limited, NEW DELHI
Prentice-Hall of Japan, Inc., TOKYO
Prentice-Hall of Southeast Asia (Pte.) Ltd., SINGAPORE

Contents

Foreword

Accounting, broadly conceived as the measurement and communication of economic information relevant to decision makers, has undergone dramatic changes during the past decade. Recent advances in quantitative methods, the behavioral sciences, and information technology are influencing current thinking in financial as well as managerial accounting. Leasing, pension plans, the use of convertible securities and warrants in mergers and acquisitions, inflation, and corporate diversification are but a few of the challenging problems facing the accountant.

These developments and the very pervasiveness of accounting activity make it difficult for teachers, students, public accountants, and financial excutives to gain convenient access to current thinking on key topics in the field. Journal articles, while current, must often of necessity give only cursory treatment or present a single point of view. Many of the important developments in the field have not crystalized to a point where they can be easily incorporated into textbooks. Further, because textbooks must necessarily limit the space devoted to any one topic, key topics often do not get the attention they properly deserve.

The Contemporary Topics series attempts to fill this gap by covering significant contemporary developments in accounting through brief, but self-contained, studies. These independent studies provide the reader with up-to-date coverage of key topics. For the practitioner, the series offers a succinct overview of developments in research and practice in areas of special interest to him. The series enables the teacher to design courses with maximum flexibility and to expose his students to authoritative analysis of controversial problems.

ALFRED RAPPAPORT

Preface

This book is concerned with the impact of the research in efficient capital markets on accounting. It is addressed to those who need or wish to know about the area, but who may not have either the time or perhaps the quantitative background to read the research that has been done.

The topic has proved to be very popular among academics and professionals with interests in economics, finance, and accounting. Much work has been done and not all of it is reviewed here. Moreover, new results appear almost daily. We were forced to stop our own examination of this evidence with what was available in July 1974. Hence, new research may have been done which modifies what is reported here. A quick check of the references will indicate whether a paper published since July 1974 was available to us (sometimes in working paper form).

We owe a great deal to many individuals who have contributed to this effort. First, we wish to single out the finance-accounting faculty and doctoral students at Cornell, all of whom made helpful suggestions. Second, we wish to thank those who have read substantial portions of this manuscript and given us helpful comments, particularly Professors Nils Hakansson of the University of California at Berkeley, Alfred

Rappaport at Northwestern, and Roland Dukes at Cornell. Additionally, we owe a major debt to the researchers who have given their time and energy to an investigation of the issues. Their names are too numerous to list here, but the reader will note many of them lurking among these pages. Our ideas and often our exposition closely reflect their work.

We also wish to express our appreciation to the administration and to the typing pool at the Graduate School of Business at Cornell who supported our efforts. Finally, we are indebted to our families who put up with such nonsense in hopes (held with diminishing conviction) that their husbands' egos, if not their financial needs, will one day be satisfied.

Any errors of omission, analysis, or fact are the sole responsibility of the authors.

Cornell University
1974

To our colleagues
in the accounting-finance doctoral seminar at Cornell University
and to those researchers
whose work made this endeavor possible.

Introduction

Is the accounting profession overly concerned with the development and application of Generally Accepted Accounting Principles (GAAP)? Has the Financial Accounting Standards Board (FASB) made a wise choice in deciding to devote its attention to technical questions such as the reporting of price-level effects and the treatment of research and development? Or should the FASB follow the Accounting Principles Board (APB) in a search for a set of principles and standards which would be the basis for both financial reporting and the related auditing function? If the former, should the FASB merely list accepted alternatives for each controversial area, or should it attempt to suggest what accounting treatment is warranted under different circumstances? If the latter, what basic theory and research methodology is appropriate and sufficiently compelling to sustain the ensuing conclusions and policy statements? For example, should published financial statements provide figures under only a single procedure (unadjusted hsitorical cost) or on several (perhaps all) accepted alternatives (price-level adjusted, if accepted, and unadjusted historical cost)? Is it sufficient to report under a single procedure if the data for other procedures can be derived from that reported?

These are a few of the issues facing accountants today. The issues are complex, and sufficient evidence (if not opinion) to provide readily acceptable answers to those engaged in accounting-policy decisions and those who must use the results does not yet exist. The need to resolve these issues has received added impetus from the SEC and the Courts in recent years. Both institutions are taking a more active role in monitoring the reporting process. In face of the present uncertainty, accountants have turned to the FASB for authoritative pronouncements that will provide guidance in auditing and attesting to published financial statements.

Currently a substantial group of academics, corporate executives, public accountants, and users of accounting statements believe that a single set of accounting standards applied uniformly to all business entities would be best. They maintain that the present policy of allowing multiple procedures in the same industry and even under similar circumstances leads to confusion and misunderstanding by the users of the information. A single set of standards would at least narrow the set of acceptable alternatives. For example, they believe an investor evaluating the reports of two firms, one of which used the first-in-first-out (FIFO) inventory valuation method while the other used the last-in-first-out (LIFO) method, might be misled by the reported earnings of the firms if the implications of the inventory valuation differences were not understood. They argue that such confusion, multiplied by the number of accounting issues in which alternative procedures are possible and by the number of financial statement users, ultimately leads to a misallocation of resources in capital markets. Most would go further to say this could occur even with one procedure if it were not carefully chosen by the appropriate policy making unit. The result in either case would be that some stocks would be overvalued compared to others. Some firms would be able to raise more capital than others, or at a lower rate of interest, even though the only real differences between the firms were their accounting reporting procedures. In effect, the use of competing accounting procedures could be responsible for major imperfections in our capital markets.

On the other hand, a significant group of persons involved with the dissemination and use of accounting information believes that the information provided by accountants not only does not have these unwanted effects but rather contributes to a better functioning of capital markets. A distinction is made between the difficulties faced by individual statement users and the aggregation of such users in the market. What may be true at the individual level may not hold at the aggregate market level. Furthermore, the reporting implications may be different depending on whether an individual user or aggregate user viewpoint is adopted.

Recent empirical research, primarily academic in its origin and principally focused on the stock market, has given rise to a theory which maintains that capital markets are generally efficient and quite sophisticated in the interpretation of financial information. What is meant when we define a market as efficient? What is the evidence pro and con concerning efficient markets? What are the implications of this evidence for the accounting profession? These are the questions to which we address ourselves in this book. Although an understanding of these issues and the relevant empirical research will not of itself provide answers to the policy questions posed earlier, it will better qualify us to seek and evaluate alternative solutions.

CHAPTER ONE

The Efficient
Market Hypothesis

In a competitive market, the equilibrium price of any good or service at a particular moment in time is such that the available supply is equated to the aggregate demand. This price represents a consensus of the members trading in the market about the true worth of the good or service, based on all publicly available information. As soon as a new piece of relevant information becomes available, it is analyzed and interpreted by the market. The result is a possible change in the existing equilibrium price. The new equilibrium price will hold until yet another bit of information is available for analysis and interpretation. For example, the performance of a few companies is considered to be heavily dependent on one individual, usually holding the position of chief executive officer. If that individual should suddenly die, the announcement of his death would probably lead to a fall in the company's stock price, especially if there were no obvious successor who could take over immediately.

1

1-1. ACCOUNTING INFORMATION AND THE SECURITIES MARKET

The market for outstanding corporate stocks appears to have the characteristics of a free and competitive market. Investors typically consider the stocks of various companies substitutes since it is not the characteristics of the issuing company which are being purchased but the opportunity for increasing one's wealth. Each stock has the potential to increase in value and thus is viewed as a substitute for any other security. This is true despite the existence of transaction costs for buying and selling shares of stocks. Although these costs restrain trading somewhat, they are, in general, small in relation to the value of the stock traded. Furthermore, they do not vary significantly from trader to trader.

The distribution system of information on corporate stocks also is consistent with a competitive market. A number of legal restrictions exist in combination with the usual competitive pressures and moral obligations to insure that corporate managers and other insiders are not selective in their dissemination of information. The existence of a large and well-established brokerage industry, an independent financial press, and a rapid and extensive communications system further assures complete retrieval, analysis, interpretation, and distribution of relevant corporate information.

Corporate news takes many forms—the announcement of a change in top management, the awarding of a large contract to a competitor, the release of a research report on the firm by a brokerage house, or a forecast of next year's earnings by the firm's president at a meeting of security analysts. The most widely used sources of information, however, are the firm's published financial reports. Representing the most commonly available source of data on past performance, these statements are used by both amateur and professional investors to predict a firm's future performance, thereby providing a base for estimating future stock prices and the related cash flows to the investor.

1-2. THE NAIVE INVESTOR ARGUMENT

A casual look at the statistics on the number of copies of annual reports distributed by various corporations and the man-hours expended by internal accountants, independent public accountants, security analysts, and investors in preparing and analyzing these reports would undoubtedly lead us to conclude that published statements play an important role in the dissemination of corporate information. However, many observers believe that, although the market pays attention to these financial statements, it frequently reacts in a naive manner to the information contained in them. This view is based on the presumption that the market is composed of a great number of individual investors, most of whom are relatively unsophisticated in their ability to understand and interpret financial statements. These naive investors, it is argued, are unable to detect subtleties in accounting reporting procedures. Thus, they often make incorrect decisions based on perceived situations or differences which are, in fact, illusory. Based on this view of individual investor behavior, it is argued that the market in total reacts naively. The result is that certain securities are at times inappropriately priced. This is a central theme, for example, in the work of one of the accounting profession's most outspoken critics, Professor Abraham Briloff of The City University of New York. In a recent book Briloff [1972] describes a number of cases which appear to show that the market was fooled by the accounting reports of publicly owned companies in that their stock prices were incorrectly set for some period of time. Whether in each case the data presented in the reports were deliberatly misrepresented to confuse investors is subject to debate. Certainly, given the plethora of complex accounting procedures and principles, we would not expect all participants in a market to be able to distinguish false or misleading information even if the information were consistently offered in the same basic format. This is one reason for requiring audited statements. But accounting information is based on numerous assumptions and principles which allow the use of alternative procedures in different situations. Examples include the timing of revenue and expense recognition and the accounting for lease obligations and mergers. This makes conclusions subject to the interpretation and analysis of the user. Furthermore, accounting information is not always presented in the same basic format, making adequate analysis of alternative investments even more difficult. Since the market is composed in substantial part of users who are relatively unsophisticated in the analysis and interpretation of accounting information, it is easy to reach the conclusion that the market in total reacts in a naive manner to financial statements.

However, there is another view, which maintains that the *total* market is quite sophisticated in the way in which it digests financial statement data and arrives at equilibrium security prices. Furthermore, this occurs in spite of the unsophisticated (or naive) nature of many if not most of the individuals who, collectively, make up the market. This view is commonly referred to, at least in academic literature, as the Efficient Market Hypothesis (EMH). A securities market is defined as efficient if (1) the prices of the securities traded in that market act as though they fully reflect all available information and (2) these prices react instantaneously, or nearly so, in an unbiased fashion to new information. We note in passing that even if the view of a sophisticated market embodied in the EMH is valid, individual investors may still make wrong decisions. Hence, the hypothesis requires "experts" (or arbitragers) of sufficient numbers or wealth to produce an efficient market. Furthermore, the hypothesis refers to the total market. It is quite possible that for a particular stock at a particular time, the hypothesis may not be true. As with all hypotheses, the EMH is an approximation of the world and those who hold this idea believe it to be substantively accurate and operationally useful.

1-3. THE DEVELOPMENT OF THE EFFICIENT MARKET HYPOTHESIS

The EMH had its genesis in the random walk theory of the movement of security prices which appeared in security price literature in the late 1950's. Actually the earliest known work on the distribution of security prices was done by Louis Bachelier [1900] who studied commodity prices in France and concluded that the current price of a commodity was also an unbiased estimate of its future price. This is the definition of a random walk as applied to the series of commodity prices, although Bachelier did not use that term. It was another sixty years before further research on security prices again suggested the hypothesis that changes in stock prices were random, that is, that they followed a random walk. Two studies published in 1959 suggested that price changes were independent of each other. One by Roberts [1959] simply showed that a series of randomly generated numbers looked very much like a series of stock prices; another by Osborne [1959] found the movement of stock prices similar to that of the movement of small particles suspended in a chemical solution. These studies ushered in a boom of research interest on this topic. Studies by Moore [1964], Granger and Morgenstern [1963], and Fama [1965A], which will be discussed in more detail in the next chapter, provided support for the tentative findings of Roberts and Osborne, and served to convince many academics, and even a few practitioners, that security prices did indeed follow a random walk. The argument that stock price changes are random does not suggest that such changes take place without cause or reason. On the contrary, prices change because of changes in the perceived earnings potential of the issuing firm or changes in the returns expected from alternative investments. In other words, the stock of knowledge on a specific security is frequently revised and updated, leading to changes in the security's price. The random walk hypothesis simply states that at a given point in time the size and direction of the next price change is random with respect to the stock of knowledge available at that point in time.

The random walk hypothesis has subsequently been referred to as the weak form of the EMH. It states that current prices fully reflect the information implied by the historical sequence of prices. In contrast, the semi-strong form of the EMH asserts that prices fully reflect *all publicly available* information. The hypothesis also has an even stronger form. If the restriction that the information be *publicly available* is removed so that the hypothesis refers to all information, then the hypothesis is referred to as the strong form of the EMH. Appendix B offers a mathematical formulation of the efficient market hypothesis.

Although the many empirical tests of the random walk hypothesis (the weak form of the EMH) provided evidence that excess profits cannot be earned simply from knowledge of past prices, no insight was provided into the economic process which was responsible for these prices. To examine this process, it is necessary to turn to the economic theory of competitive markets. As we stated at the beginning of this chapter, a competitive market will adjust the prices of its goods and services each time a new bit of information becomes available. If the market's participants become aware of this new information gradually, then the price changes will also occur gradually. This implies that successive price changes will not be independent. Thus knowledge of the size and direction of the latest change will imply something about the size and direction of the next change. On the other hand, if the market adjustment to new information is instantaneous, then these successive price changes will be independent and random.[1]

---

[1] Samuelson [1965] provides a proof that, if all available information is provided free to all market participants, and if these participants have the same investment horizon and expectations regarding prices, then market prices will fluctuate randomly. No one expects these conditions to hold exactly and Fama [1970] argues that the only requirements for random price changes are that there be no group of participants with consistently superior (or inferior) information or the ability to analyze this information and that the cost of the information not be excessive. These conditions would seem to hold for security markets in the United States today.

The Semi-Strong Form of the Efficient
Market Hypothesis

The finding that investors are unable to be superior forecasters of future prices simply by studying the series of past prices is evidence for the weak form of the efficient market hypothesis. It suggests that charting and other forms of technical analysis practiced by many investors, amateur and professional alike, is of no value. To assert that a securities market is efficient in the more useful semi-strong sense, one must demonstrate that the current prices reflect not only the information contained in the sequence of past prices but all publicly available information on the firm whose securities are being traded. Extensive tests concerned with this assertion have been conducted during the past ten years and will be discussed in the next three chapters.

We have already examined an argument that attempts to explain why the market for corporate securities might not be efficient. This was the naive-investor argument. It suggests that if market participants are relatively unsophisticated in processing accounting and other types of information, then they will be unable to arrive at prices which will impound all available information. Undoubtedly some of the information will be incorrectly interpreted and analyzed, leading to prices which are not at their appropriate equilibrium levels. But this allows superior analysts the opportunity to achieve excess profits, provided that the superior analysts can convince the naive investors, who, in turn, control enough wealth for prices to change. If the market includes a large group of professional investors who are capable of gathering, analyzing, and interpreting all types of information on the companies whose securities are being traded, then these investors will "make the markets." That is, through constant and careful attention to the market, and because of the large volume and frequency with which they trade, these professionals will insure that prices are set competitively and that they quickly (if not immediately) impound new information. Hence the conditions of an efficient market at the semi-strong level are created even in the face of a substantial number of naive investors. In this regard, Lorie and Hamilton [1973, p. 98] make an interesting point:

> There is a curious paradox. In order for the (efficient market) hypothesis to be true, it is necessary for many investors to disbelieve it. That is, market prices will promptly and fully reflect what is knowable about the companies whose shares are traded only if investors seek to earn superior returns, make conscientious and competent efforts to learn about the

companies whose securities are traded, and analyze relevant information promptly and perceptively. If that effort were abandoned, the efficiency of the market would diminish rapidly.

The EMH makes no claim concerning the rate of return which might be expected from an investment in a particular security. It asserts only that the current security price reflects all available information, thus making impossible a profit simply by knowing something about the company which others also know. This is not to say that an individual's expected average rate of return on a security investment is zero. On the contrary, the most widely held view in the finance literature today asserts that the expected return is commensurate with the risk of that investment. Thus, in an efficient market, current prices are established by the participants so that, on the average, the expected rates of return for different securities will not necessarily be the same. However, these returns should be the same for securities which exhibit the same degree of riskiness. And, in an efficient market, no investor will be able to earn an abnormal (excess) return by studying published financial reports and other sources of data which are available either to the public or at least to a large segment of the public.

1-4. CAPITAL ASSET PRICING THEORY

The theory specifying the appropriate relationships among individual stocks' expected returns which has received the widest acceptance is known as the Capital Asset Pricing Model (CAPM). This theory, developed by Sharpe [1964], Lintner [1965B], and Mossin [1966], is based on the realistic assumption that investors desire to hold securities in portfolios which are efficient in the sense that they provide a maximum return for a given level of risk.

In addition, the model was derived under the following assumptions: (1) there exists a riskless security (an asset for which the future rate of return is constant), (2) investors are able to borrow or lend unlimited amounts at this riskless rate, and (3) all investors have identical investment horizons and expectations about the distributions of the asset values at the end of this horizon. The third assumption does not mean that all investors agree about the exact value of the future price; it simply means that all investors agree about the expected value and the variability of the returns on all securities at the end of some period of time which also is identical for all investors. In others words, we do not need to assume that each and every market participant believes General

Motors will close tomorrow at $40; we only need to assume that all investors are in agreement that the distribution of GM's possible closing prices tomorrow has an expected value of $40 and a given variance.[2] The realism of these assumptions has been subjected to many challenges and we will discuss some tests of their validity in Chapter 4. For the moment, however, let us accept them as valid since these were the original assumptions used in the derivation of the CAPM.

It is not our intent here to provide the reader with a thorough background and understanding of the CAPM. There are several excellent books which explain in detail the development and nature of the model; two very readable ones are Sharpe [1970] and Lorie and Hamilton [1973]. However, in the next few paragraphs, we do hope to give the reader who is unfamiliar with the CAPM enough of an understanding for him to be able to follow our descriptions of empirical tests of the theory in the following chapters.

If the assumptions stated above hold, then investors will be concerned only with their expectations for their portfolios, and all individual securities will be evaluated with respect to their relationship to these portfolios. Thus the risk of an individual security will be its contribution to the overall portfolio risk, which is usually a value quite different from a measure of the security's total variability.

Figure 1-1 depicts graphically the investment opportunities facing an investor. The shaded region represents all possible combinations of risky securities. If an investor had to choose from only this set of portfolios, he would select one of those on the upper lefthand boundary of the shaded region since these are the only efficient portfolios. That is, these are the portfolios which provide the highest return for a given level of risk or, alternatively, the lowest risk for a given rate of return. The exact portfolio selected would depend on the investor's preferences, tastes, and financial situation.

When we add the assumption that all investors can borrow or lend at some riskless rate, L, which is determined exogenously, we increase the opportunities available. Now an investor can borrow or lend at rate L, the rate at which there is zero risk, and combine this amount with an investment in portfolio M to attain any combination on line LMN. Note that he could do the same with portfolio P; however, all portfolios on line LPQ are inferior to portfolios on LMN in that for every level of risk a higher return is attainable on line LMN than on line LPQ. By investing part of his funds at rate L and the remainder in portfolio M, an investor

---

[2] See Appendix A for a discussion of expected value, variance, and other statistical terms used in this book.

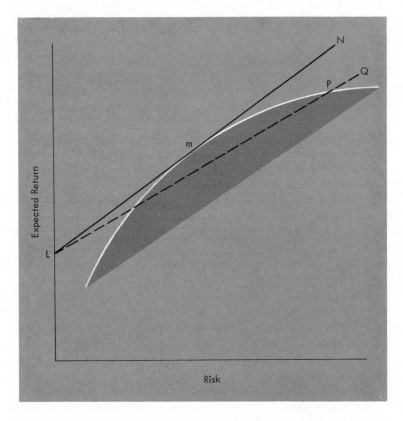

Expected Return

Risk

FIGURE 1–1

can achieve any point on the line segment *LM,* depending on the percentage invested in each component. Similarly, by borrowing at rate *L* and using these borrowed funds to increase his investment in portfolio *M,* an investor can attain any point on line segment *MN*. This borrowing procedure is called purchasing securities on margin. Each investor, again depending on his personal preferences, tastes, and financial situation, will invest the appropriate amount of funds in portfolio *M* and will borrow or lend the appropriate amount at rate *L* to attain his desired risk-return combination. An investor desiring a relatively low risk position will split his total invested funds between the riskless asset *L* and the risky portfolio *M*. An investor willing to take on more risk to obtain a higher return will borrow at the risk-free rate and invest all available funds in the risky portfolio *M*.

If we view Figure 1-1 as the set of investment opportunities available for a specific individual and attempt to aggregate these opportunities across all investors, we face the problem that individual investors will hold different beliefs about the composition of portfolio M. That is, if investors possess differing amounts of information and abilities to process this information, then their expectations about the levels of risk and return will also differ. This problem is eliminated if we make the assumption that all investors hold identical beliefs about the probability distributions of the values of each security at the end of some identical investment horizon. Under this assumption, everyone will reach the same conclusion about the composition of portfolio M, and Figure 1-1 can be viewed as representing the market.

Portfolio M comprises all the shares outstanding of all the securities in the market. Furthermore, in order that all securities be held, the prices of those securities must adjust until portfolio M contains each security in proportion to its total market value. This portfolio is called the market portfolio and the line LMN, which represents the dominant investment opportunities, is called the capital-market line. Thus the relationship between risk and return for any portfolio on the capital-market line is linear. An expected return in excess of the riskless rate L is given by the amount of risk borne by the portfolio, multiplied by the slope of the capital-market line, which is called the market price of risk.

The most frequently used measure of total risk for a security or portfolio is its standard deviation. However, this is not the risk measure which determines the expected excess return, called the risk premium. When combining securities into a portfolio, the expected portfolio return is equal to a weighted average of the expected individual security returns, where the weights are the fractions of the total dollar value of the portfolio represented by each security. However, the variance of the portfolio return is not necessarily (or usually) the weighted average of the variances of the individual security returns but is affected by the degree to which these expected returns move in concert, that is, by their covariability. And these covariances are measured as the covariances of the individual security returns with the market portfolio. Thus, when combining securities into a portfolio, the covariance of the portfolio with the market portfolio is a weighted average of the covariances of the security returns with the market portfolio. By increasing the number of securities in his portfolio, an investor is able to eliminate all of the variability of the portfolio's expected returns except that portion which is due to the covariance of the portfolio returns with the market portfolio. This is the portfolio's systematic risk, and is that part of the portfolio's total risk for which an investor can expect to be rewarded by receiving a risk premium.

For all portfolios on the capital-market line, the systematic risk equals the total risk since they include *all* securities in proportion to their total market values. For all other portfolios and individual securities, that is, for those combinations which lie below the capital-market line in Figure 1-1, the total risk includes the systematic risk and some nonsystematic or specific risk. Furthermore, it has been shown that under the assumptions stated previously this systematic risk is proportional to the expected excess return on the security or portfolio.[3]

In summary, the CAPM asserts that the expected return on any particular capital asset (security or portfolio) consists of two components —the return on a riskless security and a premium for the riskiness of the particular asset being considered. This premium is represented by an appropriate constant multiplied by the excess market return, that is, the difference between the expected return on the portfolio of *all* risky capital assets (the market return) and the return on the riskless asset. There is one appropriate constant for each security or portfolio and it represents the systematic relationship which exists between the movement of the particular asset's returns and the returns on the market portfolio. This constant is usually called the security's beta, a term derived from the statistical terminology identified with it.

The crucial aspect in the CAPM is that each security has an expected return which is related to its risk. This risk is measured by the security's systematic movements with the overall market. Furthermore, this systematic risk cannot be eliminated by merely increasing the number of securities in an investor's portfolio. On the other hand, no part of the expected return for a security is provided by that variability or price movement which is not in concert with the market since it can be eliminated by increasing portfolio diversification. In other words, the expected return is a function of the covariability of the individual security's return with the market's return.

The beta of a security or portfolio is simply the systematic risk of that capital asset, or combination of assets, expressed in units of market risk. The beta of the market portfolio is 1.0 since the covariance of a portfolio with itself is just its variance. Capital assets whose betas are less than 1.0 have less systematic risk than the overall market whereas assets with betas greater than 1.0 have more. If the expected excess return on the market portfolio during a period is 10 percent, a security with a

[3] See Sharpe [1964] or Sharpe [1970, Chapter 5].

beta of 2.0 will be expected to yield, on the average, an excess return of 20 percent. Similarly, for an expected market decline of 10 percent, the same security can be expected to lose 20 percent on the average. When observing actual returns, we find that there are differences between the observed security returns and the component explained by the market. This difference is due to the security's nonsystematic risk.

Although the CAPM is not required for the capital market to be efficient, various tests of the EMH use the CAPM in one of its several forms. Appendix B describes in more detail the assumptions and statistical forms of the CAPM.

1-5. SUMMARY

The discussion to this point has centered on the relationship between information and the market for corporate securities. Although market behavior is simply the aggregate actions of individual participants, we feel it is important to clarify the distinction between the market and the individual since the role of information, and especially published accounting reports, can be different in each context. As Beaver [1972, p. 408] states, the role of information "is two-fold: (1) to aid in establishing a set of security prices, such that there exist an optimal allocation of resources among firms and an optimal allocation of securities among investors, and (2) to aid the individual investor, who faces a given set of prices, in the selection of an optimal portfolio of securities." Beaver observes, "if we fail to make the distinction, we may be subject to any one of a number of fallacies of composition. In many cases, what is 'true' for the group as a whole is not 'true' for any individual of that group, and conversely."

In Chapter 2 we turn to a review and evaluation of the more important empirical research which lends support to the EMH, primarily in its semistrong form. Chapter 3 contains a review and critique of several studies which offer evidence contrary to the hypothesis. It is not our intent to prove or disprove the EMH in any of its forms. We believe that a more reasonable approach is not to take an extreme view of the validity of the hypothesis but rather to determine the extent to which the hypothesis holds. Chapter 4 explores some of the difficulties raised by the CAPM for conducting empirical research. Several studies of the assumptions are discussed.

In reviewing these studies we have elected to describe and critique them at a level of interest for the reader who does not do research in this area but who would profit from a summary of this evidence. The researcher involved in efficient markets needs a much deeper familiarity with these studies than can be obtained by the review which we have space to give here. This summary and evaluation is intended for those who have neither the time nor expertise to find, read, criticize, and evaluate the total impact of these studies on the EMH, accounting research, and accounting-policy questions. Additionally, we feel that there is a substantial amount of misunderstanding regarding the implications of the EMH for the accounting profession. It is this issue which we take up in Chapter 5. The reader who wishes to pursue the impact of the efficient-market literature without pausing to review the empirical research may omit Chapters 2, 3, and 4. Chapter 5 is self-contained.

CHAPTER TWO

Evidence Which Supports the Efficient Market Hypothesis

As stated in Chapter 1, the Efficient Market Hypothesis (EMH) describes a property of security prices, namely, that they reflect certain types of information instantaneously and in an unbiased fashion. Under a certain set of assumptions (zero transactions costs, free access to all available information for all market participants, and agreement among all market participants on the implications of that information for both the current set of security prices and the likelihood of certain future security prices), it can be proved that the EMH will hold. As such, these assumptions constitute a set of conditions that is sufficient for market efficiency. However, if not all of these conditions are met, then the market may not be efficient. Since it should be obvious that several of the assumptions do not strictly hold, for example, zero transactions costs, a great deal of empirical work has been conducted for the purpose of measuring the degree to which violations of these sufficient conditions cause the securities markets to be inefficient.

The EMH is difficult, if not impossible, to test directly. To do so would require a knowledge of all information relevant to the securities market plus the knowledge of how all this information should be "properly" reflected in security prices. However, it is possible to postulate some security price behavior that is implied by market efficiency. For instance, the weak form of market efficiency states that all information concerning past security prices is impounded in the present security price. This implies that no form of technical analysis (such as charting) used in selecting a portfolio of securities should consistently produce a return in excess of that required to compensate for the portfolio's risk level and any associated analysis or transactions costs. If empirical tests confirm the hypothesized return behavior for a particular type of technical analysis, then we can say that the market is efficient with respect to past security price information used in conjunction with that particular technical analysis. Further generalizations would be difficult to justify. If the empirical tests do not confirm the hypothesized behavior, the validity of the EMH is called into question. We might even conclude the EMH should be rejected. Since the EMH is an extreme hypothesis, we would not expect it to hold precisely. Thus the negative evidence of the empirical test should not cause us to immediately reject all the implications of the EMH. Because we are interested in the *degree* to which markets are efficient (or inefficient), such a negative test result should be interpreted as suggesting a limitation to the degree of efficiency. In fact, publication, and hence general knowledge, of an apparent market inefficiency might lead to its removal, as knowledgeable investors take advantage of it.

For the remainder of this chapter, we will summarize some of the empirical research which is consistent with market efficiency, that is, which describes the occurrences of behavior implied by the EMH.[1]

2-1. WEAK MARKET EFFICIENCY

As described in Chapter 1, the weak form of the EMH states that an investor cannot use past security price information to consistently earn a portfolio return in excess of the return which is commensurate with the portfolio's risk. Another way to state the hypothesis is that the investor who uses past security price data to choose his portfolio will not consistently outperform an investor who buys-and-holds a random portfolio of the same risk. In short, technical analysis alone will not yield superior portfolio performance.

---

[1] The interested reader is also referred to Beaver [1972] and Gonedes [1972], who review the evidence on market efficiency and its implications.

Much of the research into the weak form of the EMH has centered around the question of whether security prices follow a random walk. As applied to security price movements, a random walk means that the price change today is completely independent of all prior prices in all respects. The weak form of market efficiency, however, does not require all that is implied by a random walk. Rather the weak form of the EMH requires only that the expected value (or average) of today's price change is completely independent of all prior prices. For example, the observation that large price changes tend to be followed by more large price changes (but not in a *predictable* direction) would violate the random walk, but not the weak form of market efficiency. Therefore evidence which supports the random walk behavior of security prices supports the EMH. However, evidence which contradicts the random walk does not necessarily contradict the EMH.

Early Research

As mentioned in Chapter 1, the first study relating to the behavior of security prices in a competitive market was conducted at the turn of the century by Bachelier [1900], who not only developed a theory for the behavior of commodity prices, but also found that those commodity prices followed a random walk. Additional evidence that security prices followed a random walk was found by Working [1934], by Cowles and Jones [1937] and by Kendall [1953]. Although these authors were more concerned with analyzing the statistical properties of economic time-series data than with making conclusions about investment strategies, their work provides evidence of market efficiency in the weak form.

More recent research into the random walk hypothesis began in 1959 with articles by Roberts [1959] and Osborne [1959]. Roberts compared the levels of the Dow Jones industrial average with the levels of a variable generated by a random walk mechanism and concluded that the random walk mechanism produced patterns very similar to the patterns of stock price movements.

Roberts showed that a series of cumulative random numbers will closely resemble an actual stock price series. This is illustrated in Figures 2–1 and 2–2 taken from his work. He further showed that changes in the random number series, as expected, do not exhibit a pattern as is true for stock price changes. This is illustrated in Figures 2–3 and 2–4.

Osborne found that security prices behaved in a manner similar to that known to physicists as Brownian motion. Brownian motion describes the movement of particles in solution, where movements of different magnitudes may occur at any time, independent of any prior movements.

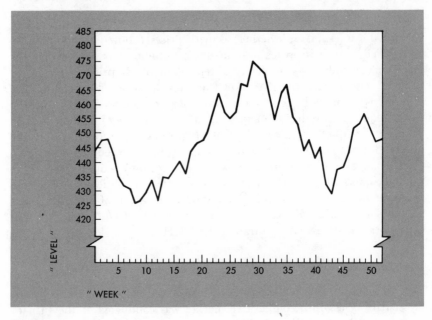

FIGURE 2–1

Simulated market level

   Source: Roberts [1959], p. 5.

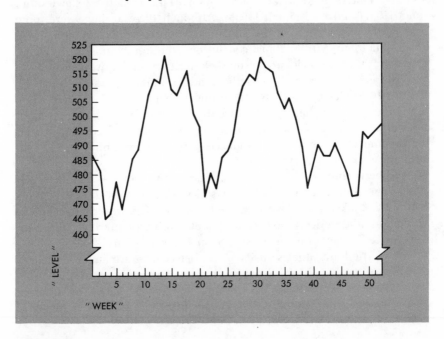

FIGURE 2–2

Actual Friday closing levels, 12/30/55–
12/28/56, Dow Jones industrial index

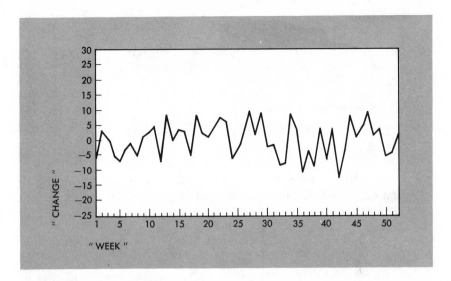

FIGURE 2–3

Simulated market changes

Source: Roberts [1959], p. 5.

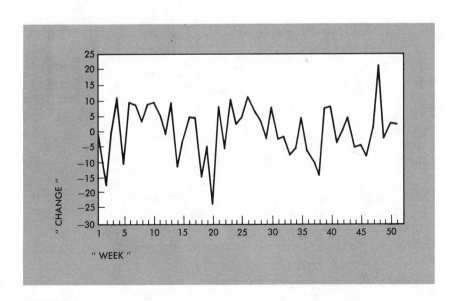

FIGURE 2–4

*Actual changes from Friday to Friday (closing) 1/6/56–
12/28/56, Dow Jones industrial index*

Source: Roberts [1959], p. 5.

So defined, Brownian motion is a particular type of random walk. Osborne found that security prices behaved in a manner consistent with a Brownian motion model in which the price change in one period was independent of the price change in any preceding period.

Serial Correlation Studies

After the appearance of the Roberts and Osborne articles, a number of additional studies appeared which attempted to test whether security prices followed a random walk. Moore [1964] looked at the serial correlation of weekly security prices. Serial correlation is a measure of the association of a series of numbers separated by some constant time period, such as the association of the level of Gross National Product in one year with the level of Gross National Product in the previous year. In particular, Moore measured the correlation of one week's price change with the next week's price change. He found an average serial correlation of − 0.06 which might indicate a very slight tendency for security price changes to reverse themselves, that is, for a price rise to follow a price fall and vice versa. However, the evidence is so weak that it cannot be interpreted as being different from an average correlation of zero, which implies no association at all. Further, the existence of such a price reversal system of the strength implied by a correlation coefficient of − 0.06 would not allow sufficient returns to compensate for the transactions costs involved.

Fama [1965A] tested the serial correlation of daily price changes for the thirty firms composing the Dow Jones industrial average for five years prior to 1962. While he found an average serial correlation of 0.03, this result, like Moore's, is not sufficiently far from zero to indicate that any correlation exists between price changes in successive periods. Fama also used *runs* tests to see whether price changes were likely to be followed by more price changes of the same sign. He found a slight tendency for this to occur, but again the results were insufficient to reject the random walk hypothesis (or the weak form of the EMH). A similar analysis was conducted by Hagerman and Richmond [1973] for the price changes of securities traded in the over-the-counter market. Since the types of securities and trading mechanisms vary from market to market, we must keep in mind that efficiency of the New York Stock Exchange does not imply that other securities markets are also efficient. However, Hagerman and Richmond did find that the returns of over-the-counter securities were not serially correlated.

Another study of the efficiency of a market other than securities was conducted by Black and Scholes [1972] who tested the efficiency of the option market. (In the option market, participants trade in contracts which give one the option to sell at a specified price [a "put"] or to buy at a specified price [a "call"], within a specified length of time.) Black and Scholes found that there was significant mispricing of the option contracts, but the transactions costs were so high that there was no opportunity for traders to earn an abnormal return by taking advantage of mispricing.

A statistical technique called spectral analysis was used by Granger and Morgenstern [1963] to test the randomness of stock prices. Spectral analysis can be used to find more complex relationships between stock returns in different periods than could be found using the simple serial correlation technique employed by previous researchers. Nevertheless, Granger and Morgenstern, detecting no substantial relationship between one period's security returns and the returns in prior periods, concluded that security prices follow a random walk.

Technical Analysis Studies

Some proponents of technical analysis (those who use past security prices to predict future price changes) claimed that the serial correlation tests were too narrow, and that such tests did not prove that more complex strategies could not use past price data to earn an abnormal rate of portfolio return. In addition, they argued that the lack of statistical significance in serial correlations might not correspond to a lack of economic significance in price changes.

Alexander [1961] used a filter rule technique to see if an abnormal return could be earned using past price data. A filter rule works in the following way. If a stock's price advances by a certain percentage over a previous low point, it is bought. If the stock declines from a previous high point, it should be sold when the decline exceeds a specified percentage. Alexander found that his filter rules produced very large rates of return, particularly for small filters (for example, five percent). However, when transactions costs are considered, the abnormal returns disappear for all filter rules. Further research into the use of filter rules by Fama [1965A] and Fama and Blume [1966] failed to show an abnormal rate of return for the filter rules studied.

In summary, Alexander's results contradicted the random walk hypothesis, that security changes are independent of prior price changes, but did not disprove the weak form of the EMH, that such dependencies may not be used to earn an abnormal portfolio return.

Another technical analysis procedure was proposed by R. Levy [1967]. Using a relative strength method based on the ratio of a stock's current price to its average price, he found a rule which yielded an abnormal portfolio return. However, Jensen [1967] pointed out that Levy had tested his technical model on the same data that were used to select the model, which of course biased the test results in favor of the model. When Jensen and Bennington [1970] tested Levy's procedure on other sets of data, no significant abnormal return was found.

2-2. SEMI-STRONG MARKET EFFICIENCY

The semi-strong form of the EMH states that security prices will always reflect publicly available information. In other words, information, such as the announcement of a firm's most recent earnings forecast, will be immediately impounded in the firm's security price. Therefore, it would be impossible for an investor to earn a portfolio return, based on this publicly available information, in excess of the return which is commensurate with the portfolio risk.

What are the implications of semi-strong market efficiency for accounting? If semi-strong market efficiency holds, then there is no reason to suspect that the visibility of certain accounting information will affect stock prices so long as it is reported. For instance, an item which is only disclosed in a footnote, or perhaps in a 10-K report to the Securities and Exchange Commission, will be impounded in security prices just as surely as if it were in the main body of the financial statements.

Tests of the semi-strong form of the EMH have studied the reaction of security prices to various types of information around the announcement time of that information. If the market is efficient in the semi-strong sense, we would expect the following type of security price behavior surrounding a public announcement. If the announcement had some economic significance, then there should be some reaction; however, the EMH would predict that this reaction would occur prior to or almost immediately upon the public announcement. Since the information may be learned by the investment community from alternative information sources prior to its public announcement, the existence of a price reaction prior to the public announcement would not be unusual. Furthermore, a reaction immediately upon the announcement date could be caused by any additional information not anticipated by or disclosed to the market participants. However, the semi-strong form of the EMH would predict that there could be a sharp price change on the announcement of new information, but no discernible price reaction following the announcement, because the market participants would adjust market prices immediately (or nearly so) and in an unbiased manner, thereby removing any possibility for future abnormal returns.

Market Reaction Tests

The first such study of the semi-strong form of the EMH was conducted by Fama, Fisher, Jensen, and Roll [1969], who considered the behavior of abnormal security returns at the announcement of stock splits. Since stock splits are frequently associated with increased dividend payouts, it would be expected that split announcements would contain some economic information. Fama et al. found that there was considerable market reaction *prior* to the split announcement. In fact, the average cumulative abnormal security return for the thirty month period up to the month of announcement was in excess of 30 percent. This figure represents a return significantly above a normal rate of return, that is, the return from buying-and-holding a portfolio of similar risk.

However, the behavior of the security prices *after* the split announcement was exactly what the EMH would predict. Following the public announcement, no more extraordinary returns could be achieved based on the knowledge of the split. The average cumulative abnormal return, which was increasing prior to the announcement, ceased to increase (or decrease) significantly in the periods following the split announcement.

A study by Scholes [1972] observed security price reaction to the offering of secondary stock issues. Scholes found that the security price declined when the issuer was a corporation or corporate officer, indicating that the market viewed such an offering as containing bad news. On the other hand, secondary offerings by individuals, banks and insurance companies, and estates and trusts (perhaps less likely to be selling on the basis of bad news than corporate officials) were viewed in a less negative fashion: the security price did not decline significantly. Price changes associated with the secondary offerings were permanent and occurred within six days of the issue. This price behavior of secondary issues lends support to the EMH contention that the market adjusts to new information quickly and in an unbiased manner.

A similar study by Kraus and Stoll [1972] examined the effects of large block trades on the behavior of security prices. They found that there was a temporary effect on share price associated with the block trade. Trades which were seller-initiated were characterized by a decrease in price, but the price rapidly recovered, and by the end of the day the recovery was complete (although the price did not return to the preblock level, presumably because the market perceived some negative information in the trade). Mirror-image price behavior characterized block trades that were buyer-initiated. In either case, there was no predictable price behavior after the day on which the block trade occurred, which is consistent with the semi-strong form of the EMH.

Another type of announcement that has been examined is the announcement of changes in dividends. Two studies, one by Pettit [1972] and one by Watts [1973], measured the market's reaction to dividend announcements. Although the authors reached different conclusions concerning the importance of dividend changes to market participants, the results of both studies are consistent with the behavior implied by the EMH: there was no evidence that a firm's dividend announcement affected the firm's security price in the periods following the announcement.

Waud [1970] examined the size and direction of stock price changes surrounding the announcement of changes in the Federal Reserve discount rate. While the price changes on the announcement days were significant and in the predicted direction (for example, a price decrease with an increase in the discount rate), there was no indication that the price changes persisted beyond a couple of days after the announcement. In fact, there was some evidence that the market anticipated the announcement by a few days.

Market Reaction to Accounting Numbers

A number of tests of the EMH, with varying forms and results, have a more direct connection with accounting.

Ball and Brown [1968] used a procedure similar to that used by Fama et al. to assess the behavior of security prices when a firm's annual earnings were announced in *The Wall Street Journal*. Ball and Brown reasoned that the market participants would have formed opinions reflected in their forecasts of what the earnings numbers should be, and, collectively, these forecasts would be reflected in a market forecast of the stock's price. They further reasoned that the reaction of a stock's price would reflect the difference between the firm's actual earnings and the market's forecast. Accordingly, Ball and Brown formed estimates of the market's earnings forecast and then evaluated a security price reaction to the good news of actual earnings in excess of the forecast and to the bad news of actual earnings short of the forecast. This reaction was measured as though the market participant had access to good or bad news prior to the availability of this news to the market. The measure accumulated the excess return that could be made over the time period prior to the announcement date. In the case of good news, the average cumulative abnormal return began to rise twelve months prior to the actual annual earnings announcement, due to alternative sources of information, such as interim reports. By the time of the announcement, the average excess return had reached about 7.5 percent. A mirror image of the same behavior was observed in the case of bad news, with the average cumulative abnormal return reaching −10 percent by the announcement of annual earnings. In both cases (good or bad news), the cumulative excess return displayed no significant behavior in the months following the earnings announcement. This study indicates that there is a correlation between earnings numbers and security returns, but that this earnings information is quickly impounded in security prices in an unbiased manner. In other words, the results are consistent with the semi-strong form of the EMH. Brown and Kennelly [1972] found similar results concerning the market reaction to quarterly earnings reports. (See also Benston [1967] and [1973].) Figure 2–5 illustrates Ball and Brown's findings for the good news and bad news cases.

Announcement Effects

A study by Beaver [1968] yields some insights into the speed with which the information in annual earnings announcements is impounded in security prices. Beaver examined the size of price changes and levels of trading volume in the weeks surrounding the announcement of a firm's annual earnings in *The Wall Street Journal*. He found that the absolute values of the price changes and the levels of trading were significantly higher during the announcement week than any other week. In addition, price changes and volume in the week following the announcement week returned to pre-announcement levels. While this research does not provide any definite conclusions concerning the lack of bias in the market's assessment of new information, it does provide substantive evidence that the reaction occurs quickly, one of the characteristics of market efficiency. Similar results were found for the duration of announcement effects for quarterly earnings by May [1971] who used weekly price data for firms traded on the American Stock Exchange, and by Jordan [1973] who used daily price data for a sample of firms from Forbes' *21st Annual Report on American Industry*. Figure 2–6 summarizes Beaver's results.

Another type of announcement was studied by Patz and Boatsman [1972] who examined the market reaction to the Accounting Principles Board's 22 October 1971 release of a memorandum concerning the cost center used by oil companies as a basis for accumulating certain material

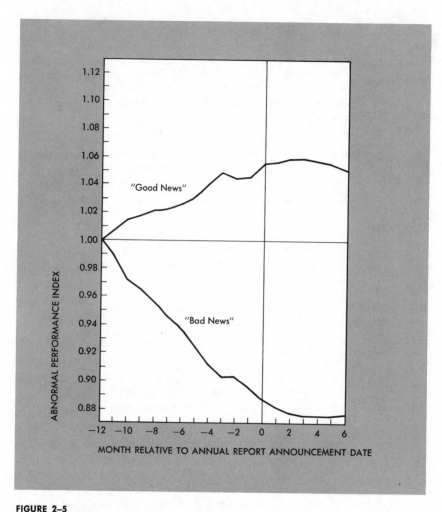

FIGURE 2–5

Abnormal performance indexes for various portfolios:
Price behavior for stocks with good news and bad news

Source: Ball and Brown [1968], p. 169.

costs. While the memorandum caused an extensive reaction, particularly among oil companies, Patz and Boatsman found no significant market reaction to the announcement, consistent with the EMH that the market perceived the proposed changes as bookkeeping changes with no economic impact.

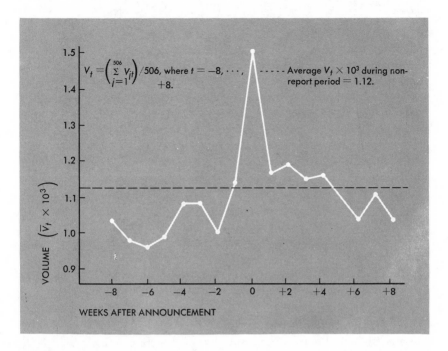

FIGURE 2–6

Volume stock trading

Source: Beaver [1968], p. 89.

Foster [1973] examined the market's reaction to preliminary earnings estimates made by company officials. He found that investors reacted quickly to the announcements, since volume levels increased during the week of announcement, but returned to preannouncement levels immediately after the announcement week. Further, the results indicate a price change accompanies the announcement, but this price change occurs quickly, leaving no opportunity for an abnormal return in the period following the announcement week.

Accounting Procedure Changes

In addition to tests of the market reaction to accounting earnings numbers, other researchers have attempted to assess the impact on security prices of changes in accounting techniques. Many of the changes in a firm's external reporting procedures do not signify a change in the economic condition of the firm, unlike changes in reporting for tax purposes.

Therefore, external reporting changes, such as a change from accelerated to straight-line depreciation or from LIFO to FIFO inventory valuation (for book purposes only), have no impact on the economic condition of the firm and therefore should have no effect on security prices in an efficient market.

A contrary hypothesis, known as the **Naive Investor Hypothesis** (NIH), has been advanced by some authors, for example, Sterling [1970]. The NIH states that investors are conditioned to react to, say, an accounting earnings number and may continue to react in the same manner even if the measurement method underlying the earnings number changes. Although some individual investors may react in a naive fashion, the existence of a few sophisticated investors, who have access to large amounts of capital, may be sufficient to guarantee market efficiency. Therefore, naive behavior at the individual level does not necessarily imply naive behavior at the market level. However, if the NIH does occur at the market level (a violation of the EMH), we would expect to observe security price changes associated with the accounting changes.

At first, the empirical studies in this area focused on earnings capitalization models (which express security prices as a function of earnings), in order to assess whether the process of earnings measurement had any effect on the earnings capitalization function. Mlynarczyk [1969] used a sample of electric utility companies to determine whether a firm's method of tax-allocation accounting (normalization, flow-through) affected the firm's earnings capitalization function. Mlynarczyk did find a significant effect attributable to the method of accounting for taxes, so that the market did not naively interpret the earnings numbers generated by the alternative procedures as equivalent. However, when Mlynarczyk attempted to determine whether the market made a proper adjustment for the differing accounting methods, he concluded that this was not the case. Unfortunately, Mlynarczyk chose his sample from an industry where the accounting method might have an economic impact on the firm, since it is possible that tax-allocation accounting could affect the behavior of a regulatory commission and therefore temporarily affect a utility's cash flows. This sample problem, coupled with some statistical shortcomings reduces the strength of Mlynarczyk's results concerning the proper adjustment by the market for differing accounting methods. A similar study by Gonedes [1969] encompassed a broader sample of firms and a larger number of alternative accounting procedures, with results that were much more ambiguous than those of Mlynarzyk concerning the effects of accounting procedures on the earnings capitalization function.

Other authors have examined the effect of accounting procedure on the price-earnings ratio (PE ratio), which is actually a variant of the earnings capitalization model. O'Donnell [1965, 1968] studied the effects of deferral versus flow-through accounting for taxes on the PE ratios of electric utilities. O'Donnell found that the method of accounting exerted an effect, but, as in the Mlynarczyk study, without analysis of the effect of accounting method on the behavior of regulatory commissions.

Comiskey [1971] looked at the PE ratios of a set of steel firms before and after a switch from accelerated to straight-line depreciation for book purposes and compared these ratios to the PE ratios of a control group of steel firms which did not switch accounting procedures. While the PE ratios of the control group generally increased over the period, the ratios of the firms who switched accounting procedures generally declined. Thus it would seem that the higher earnings that resulted from the accounting change were not interpreted naively by the market.

A major shortcoming of all the above studies is that they employ the dividend (earnings) capitalization model of security prices. This model is essentially a "certainty" model, and its use in an uncertain environment is tenuous at best. Since there is no explicit consideration of risk, Comiskey's findings, for example, could be the result of risk changes that Ball [1972] found to be associated with accounting changes.

A more sophisticated analysis was conducted by Archibald [1972] who observed the market reaction to changes from accelerated to straight-line depreciation for book purposes. Since this accounting change would have the effect of increasing reported income numbers, it could, under the NIH, lead to increased security prices. On the other hand, the EMH would predict that no significant price change would occur since the accounting change does not represent an economic change. While there were patterns in Archibald's results that could be interpreted as a market reaction to the accounting change, none of the observed patterns were large enough to be statistically significant. Hence, Archibald could not reject the hypothesis that the observed patterns were merely the result of random behavior.

In a similar manner, Kaplan and Roll [1972] studied the effect of changes in accounting for the investment credit and in depreciation methods. While Kaplan and Roll did find some evidence that there was a significant market reaction to changes in the accounting procedure for the investment credit, their conclusion must be tempered due to statistical problems. As a result, the Kaplan and Roll study should probably be treated as supporting the semi-strong form of the EMH. This study will be reexamined in Chapter 3, which reviews studies with results contrary to the EMH.

Recently, Ball [1972] studied the market behavior surrounding several types of changes in accounting procedures. While Ball found that the firms in his sample did experience changes in their risk characteristics, there was no evidence of an abnormal return in the months surrounding the accounting changes.

Sunder [1973] examined the market reaction to changes in inventory valuation method. In particular, firms which switched to LIFO (last in-first out) inventory valuation experienced an increase in stock price (on average) during the months up to the accounting change. (Since adoption of LIFO decreases taxes in periods of rising prices, this reaction would be expected since it constitutes an economic event.) After the accounting change no abnormal price behavior could be discerned.

In summary, we have reviewed some of the literature which lends support to the semi-strong form of the EMH. We now turn to the evidence available on the strong form of market efficiency.

2-3. STRONG MARKET EFFICIENCY

The strong form of the EMH states that all information will be impounded in security prices in such a way as to leave no opportunity for extraordinary returns based on any information. In Chapter 1 we noted that the EMH is an extreme hypothesis and that we would not expect it to hold exactly, and this is especially the case with the strong form of the hypothesis.

Of course, if the strong form of the EMH did hold, the security prices would always reflect *all* relevant information, regardless of what information was publicly available. Therefore, any policy change with regard to accounting disclosure would have no effect on security prices, although it could affect the portfolio decisions made by individual investors. However, almost all of the available evidence indicates that the strong form of market efficiency does not hold.

An interesting test of the strong form of the EMH is provided by Collins [1975]. The Securities and Exchange Commission required that, beginning with years ending on or after 31 December 1970, all registrants engaged in more than one line of business must report sales and profits by product line in their 10-K report. Furthermore, the 1970 10-K report filings were required to contain this information for the years 1967–1969 for comparison. Consequently, Collins had access to historical segment earnings data for the years 1967–1969 which previously were not available to the general public. These segment earnings data are important because, as Collins shows, future consolidated earnings of multiproduct firms are more accurately predicted using segment revenue and profit data than by using historical consolidated earnings data. Given this finding, Collins formulated a test of the strong form of the EMH by adopting a strategy similar to that used by Ball and Brown [1968]. He formed two sets of estimates of annual earnings for 92 multiproduct firms for the years 1968, 1969, and 1970. The first set used the historical segment data and the second used only the historical consolidated numbers. His trading rule was to buy stock of those companies for which the segment-based earnings forecast exceeded the consolidated-based forecast and to sell short the stock of those firms for which the segment-based earnings forecast was less than the consolidated-based forecast. He used the market model to eliminate the market related movements in the stock prices and found that in both 1968 and 1969 this trading rule would have earned a statistically significant abnormal return. However, this finding could not be replicated for the 1970 data. Thus, the market was not efficient with respect to the *non-public* segment revenue and profit data of multiproduct firms, for these data could be used to anticipate changes in total entity earnings which would otherwise be unexpected.

Mutual Fund Performance

The one area in which there is some support for the strong form of the EMH is in the performance of mutual funds. It might be argued that the managers of mutual funds would be more likely than the average investor to have access to insider information, that is, information not otherwise publicly available. If this is the case, and such information can be used to earn extraordinary returns, then we would expect mutual funds (or at least some mutual funds) to consistently achieve a higher than average performance.

The performance of mutual funds has been studied by a number of authors. Friend, et al. [1962] studied 189 funds from December 1952 to September 1958. Sharpe [1966] measured the performance of 36 mutual funds from 1954 to 1963. A more comprehensive study of 115 mutual funds from 1955 to 1964 was conducted by Jensen [1969]. Finally, Friend, Blume, and Crockett [1970] studied 136 mutual funds from 1960 into 1969, and Williamson [1972] studied 180 mutual funds from 1961 to 1970. Although the samples of firms, time periods, and performance measures differed somewhat between these studies, their results were remarkably similar. On the average, mutual funds did no better than an individual investor would expect if he purchased a diversified portfolio of similar risk. In fact, when all of the funds' expenses are considered, a majority of funds did worse than a randomly selected portfolio would have done. There is, of course, a possibility that a few funds could consistently earn an extraordinary return, but there is as yet no empirical work to document the existence of such funds.

Given the evidence contrary to the strong form of the EMH, the mutual fund performance studies probably do not indicate that insider information is always impounded in market prices. An alternative and more probable conclusion is that no one mutual fund has consistent first access to insider or nonpublic information. Since the numerous mutual funds are all competing for such information, it is not surprising that on the average, these funds do no better than an average performance, that is, average with respect to all other mutual funds in the market.

2-4. SUMMARY

In this chapter, we have reviewed a selected set of the literature which lends support to the efficient market hypothesis. In keeping with our purpose for this book, the reader should not conclude at this point that the EMH does hold, just as, after reading Chapter 3, he should resist concluding that it does not. The truth, we feel, lies somewhere between. What we need to learn is the extent or degree to which the EMH does hold. The evidence reviewed here describes situations in which the EMH does seem to hold. Whereas no general conclusions about the degree of market efficiency may yet be made, the cited evidence may affect our expectations that the EMH will hold in similar situations.

CHAPTER THREE

Evidence Which
Questions the Efficient
Market Hypothesis

Although our summary in Chapter 2 suggested an unusual degree of support for the semi-strong form of the Efficient Market Hypothesis (EMH), there is also a set of studies whose results are inconsistent with it. We do not suggest that these studies necessarily lead to rejection of the EMH, but, rather, that a decision as to the extent of one's confidence in the hypothesis requires that all results be acknowledged and their combined impact considered. Such studies may be discredited or overwhelmed (and they do have their problems), but they should not simply be ignored. The main purpose of this chapter is to acknowledge these studies and briefly present their conclusions.

As we observed in Chapter 2, the EMH is difficult, if not impossible, to test directly. Hence empirical studies are based on the implications of the hypothesis and the conditions necessary for it to be true. These conditions are:

3-1. Condition One: Association of Returns: The excess return to a security in the next period should not be associated in a predictable way with the excess returns of any other period.[1]

3-2. Condition Two: Expected Excess Returns: Any security trading scheme based on information available to the market has a zero expected excess return.

3-3. Condition Three: Existence of Superior Trading Strategies: If the expected return is non-negative, then no mechanical trading rule can have a greater expected return than a simple buy-and-hold strategy.[2]

3-4. Condition Four: Instantaneous and Unbiased Response: The market response to the formal issuance of publicly available information (such as dividend or stock-split announcements) should be instantaneous and unbiased.[3]

These implications may be summarized by describing the security return series as a "fair game" in which the expected excess returns based on publicly available information are zero. Expected excess returns must include an allowance for search and transaction costs associated with a particular trading scheme. Further, the returns obtained must be considered in light of the risk of the portfolio held.

Before accepting the negative findings reported here, the reader must consider the limitations of the research discussed. These limitations will be described for each study or group of studies. Further, the reader will recall that the EMH is an extreme hypothesis, and we should not expect it to be literally true. The weight of these studies points more to a questioning of the degree of efficiency of the EMH than to a total rejection of it. Finally, the discovery of an inefficiency may lead to its elimination as knowledgeable investors exploit it. This is one means by which an efficient market can prevail.

3-1. ASSOCIATION OF RETURNS: (CONDITION ONE)

A study by Ying [1966], using daily data on the Standard and Poor's 500 stock index and the NYSE aggregate volume, seems to provide evi-

[1] In formalistic terms this implies that the return series can be described as a martingale and, if so, the serial covariances of the return series for a security should be zero for all lags. The EMH rules out more than this, however. It also rules out nonlinear dependencies on which superior trading strategies can be built (see Condition Three) even though they exhibit zero trading covariance.

[2] If expected returns are negative, an optimal trading rule may be to hold cash.

[3] These four conditions are not independent of one another. However, they suggest the somewhat different means by which tests have been made. Categorizing the studies is merely a useful means of reporting the results.

dence that is contrary to the EMH. Ying used an analysis of variance technique to study the effects of three factors on the change in the value of the S&P index on day $t+1$. These three factors were: the change in the value of the S&P index on day t, the NYSE volume on day t, and the change in the NYSE volume on day t.

Among other results Ying found that a fall in the daily S&P price is followed, on the average, by a further fall in price; similar conditions also hold for a price increase. This implies that the S&P index in period t is associated with the S&P index in period $t+1$.

Granger and Morgenstern [1970, p. 204] argue that the adjustments Ying made to avoid the effects of aggregate dividend changes on the S&P price series produce the results he obtained. They claim Ying's adjustment process induces autocorrelation that is sufficient to explain his results. Although they seem to have misinterpreted the method Ying used to adjust the price and volume series,[4] Granger and Morgenstern's demonstration that Ying's adjustments induce autocorrelation remains valid and may partially explain his results.[5] It is not clear, however, that this criticism totally accounts for Ying's findings.[6] More important, it also has not

---

[4] Ying used Standard and Poor's index and NYSE volume figures, and adjusted them for aggregate dividend rates and outstanding shares respectively. Because daily figures were not available for these adjustment factors, Ying used the linear interpolation formula

$$P'(t) = \frac{P(t)}{a + t\left(\dfrac{b-a}{n}\right)}$$

for the price series, where $P'(t)$ is the adjusted price, n the number of trading days in the month, and a and b are the dividend rates at time $t=0$ and $t=n$, respectively. A similar adjustment was used for the volume series. Granger and Morgenstern argue that the adjustment model was

$$P'(t) = \frac{P(t)}{ta + (n-t)b}.$$

However, in personal correspondence Ying has stated to us that he used the former interpolation formula.

[5] Serial correlation may also be attributed to the method used to compute the Standard and Poor index. They use the last price available at the close of a trading day, which may be the price recorded at a much earlier time than the close for a low-volume day.

[6] Downes in some as yet unpublished research has replicated Ying's work attempting to avoid some of the previous difficulties mentioned by Granger and Morgenstern and using more recent data. He found that price changes in period t were related to price changes in the previous period and to the interactions between price changes and both volume and volume changes in the previous period. Also Ying used spectral analysis to find a significant relationship between the direction of price movements and lagged volume statistics, but Downes was unable to verify these results in his replication efforts. Finally, it is possible that Ying's results may be due to the particular order in which his variables were tested using the analysis-of-variance technique (the statistical testing procedure used by the author).

been established that profitable trading rules over and above transactions costs can be formulated on Ying's results, even to the extent they hold: the price changes may be inadequate to cover the associated search and transaction costs, so condition three would still hold.

Another study which tested for dependencies in aggregate market data was performed by Philippatos and Nawrocki [1973]. They used successive daily values of the proportions of the securities whose prices advanced, declined, and remained unchanged on the NYSE for the period 1 October 1963 to 30 September 1971 and looked for evidence of temporal dependencies which could be used for forecasting overall market movements. Their basic methodology was adopted from a study by Fama [1965B], who performed similar tests on data from the period 2 June 1952 to 29 October 1962. Both studies used various exponential forecasting prediction rules of the form

$$p_{it} = aq_{i,t-1} + (1-a)\, \bar{q}_i$$

where p_{it} is tomorrow's value of proportion i, $i=1,2,3$, for advances, declines, and remains unchanged, respectively,

$q_{i,t-1}$ is today's value of proportion i,

$\bar{q}_i$ is the long run average of proportion i, and

a and $(1-a)$ are the appropriate weights.

Fama found a to be approximately 0.22 and considered it to be too small for reliable forecasting. On the other hand, Philippatos and Nawrocki estimated a as 0.32 and argued that forecasting rules of this form "can be helpful in predicting the successive proportions of securities advancing, declining, and remaining unchanged" [p. 458]. However, the authors do not provide any evidence that profitable trading rules can be developed using these findings.

A study by Cheng and Deets [1971] questions whether successive price changes are mutually stochastically independent rather than just pairwise independent. (The former condition is required by the EMH.) Cheng and Deets conclude that dependence exists by finding evidence which is contrary to certain conditions which follow from the assumption of mutual stochastic independence. Their tests also imply that a rebalancing strategy, in which the portfolio is adjusted at each period so there is an equal dollar investment in each security, leads to superior returns over a buy-and-hold strategy. Unfortunately, the authors included neither transaction costs nor taxes in their study, and hence it may be possible to show that the net return is still consistent with the EMH (that is, superior returns cannot be made using this information) even if the study is otherwise valid.

Goldman [1975] finds three flaws in the Cheng and Deets argument. First, one of their four tests is formulated incorrectly. Second, the skewed nature of the return distributions makes the significance of the empirical results of the four tests extremely difficult if not impossible to determine. And third, their sampling technique is biased in favor of their observed results. Their empirical tests use returns on the thirty *current* Dow Jones industrials for the years 1937–1969, which systematically excludes all bankruptcies and failures and induces a negative serial correlation. Their neglect of dividends may tend to induce negative serial correlation as well.

Moreover, West and Tinic [1973, p. 735], using Smidt's work [1968], suggest that "the cost associated with purchasing the services of market makers permits the existence of small price dependencies that would otherwise be eliminated by arbitrage. More importantly, however, this cost encourages the reversals—that is, negative serial dependencies which tend to enhance the profitability of a rebalancing strategy, particularly under the assumption that transaction costs do not have to be paid." But someone with a reasonably sophisticated view of the economic nature of the expected returns model (vs. Cheng and Deets' statistical formulation) would expect these negative serial correlations, that is, the Cheng and Deets results should be anticipated. The implications of market inefficiency are less striking than they initially appear.

3-2. EXPECTED EXCESS RETURNS: (CONDITION TWO)

McWilliams [1966] attempted to use the price-earnings ratio as an analytical tool for stock selection by analyzing investment returns on securities selected from the COMPUSTAT population.[7]

Based on a sample of 390 firms McWilliams showed that, on the average, low price-earnings portfolios yielded a higher return than high price-earnings portfolios. In order to emphasize this point, the author showed the investment results for $10,000 invested on April 30, 1952 in various price-earnings deciles, assuming reinvestment on an annual basis in the same decile for the next twelve years. His results showed that the $10,000 would have grown to:

[7] The COMPUSTAT data base contains detailed financial statistics on a large sample of American and Canadian corporations. It is maintained by Investors Management Services, Denver, Colorado.

$45,329 if invested in the highest decile,

$103,960 if invested in the lowest decile, and

$50,236 if invested in the Dow Jones industrial average.

Unfortunately, again no adjustments were made for risk and transactions costs. Also we observe that the Dow does not include dividends, whereas McWilliams' portfolios do.

However, given the data in McWilliams' study, it is possible to get an idea as to the magnitude of risk. Computing Sharpe's [1966] reward-to-variability ratio, it appears that these ratios vary substantially across the ten 39-stock portfolios. However, the reward-to-variability ratio for the lowest decile (lowest price-earnings) portfolio is about 60% higher than that for the highest decile portfolio and approximately 22% higher than for the entire sample. This implies that McWilliams' low price-earnings portfolios outperform (using the Sharpe criterion) his high price-earnings portfolios. Further, and more important, if his entire sample is sufficiently representative of market-based portfolios (there are COMPUSTAT biases against this including size, age, the nonfailed nature of the sample firms, etc.), then low price-earnings portfolios may also outperform the market. The implication is that superior trading rules can be based on PE ratios, a violation of condition three, if valid.

A study by Miller and Widmann [1966] is similar to that of Mc-Williams. Miller and Widmann computed percentage price appreciation for a sample of COMPUSTAT firms with sales exceeding $150 million, and assumed holding periods of one, three, and five years. Based on their results, the authors [p. 26] state that "the low price-earnings group has consistently outperformed the high price-earnings group. In fact there is a distinct tendency for the groups to fall in a pattern of inverse rank correlation with the height of the P/E ratio." In order to verify that the better performance of the low price-earnings group was not caused by a few securities, the authors examined the distribution of price appreciation in the lowest and highest price-earnings quintiles. They found the two distributions to be almost identical. The authors concluded [p. 28]:

> The results we have found in our relative price performance studies point to a degree of irrationality in the stock market, at least so over the span of years studied. Furthermore, if irrationality exists, the market is inefficient in its role as an allocator of capital funds. One would expect that prices of equities would move in accord with earnings prospects if the market were efficient. It is logical then that companies with superior earnings prospects would sell at a premium in an efficient market, as we found to be generally true. It is possible, however, that the premiums on growth

stocks could be too large. If so, an inefficiency exists in the market the same as if growth stocks were evaluated with too small a premium or with no premium at all over non-growth stocks. We feel that evidence uncovered in our empirical studies supports the contention that the prospects of growth situations are often evaluated too liberally and that investor prejudice and distrust create large areas of underevaluation.

This study suffers from the same limitations inherent to the McWilliams study and, in addition, from the assumption that earnings data were available on the reporting date.[8] A NYSE firm's earnings numbers typically are available to the market with sufficient accuracy upon the announcement in *The Wall Street Journal* of the preliminary report of income and sales data. This occurs after the reporting date.

In a more recent study Basu [1974] again examined the possibility of achieving excess returns using price-earnings data. Basu found first that "during the period April 1957-March 1971, the performance of low price-earnings securities was significantly different (better) from that of high price-earnings securities: the low price-earnings portfolios seem to have systematically earned returns in *excess* of that implied by their levels of risk . . . ; in contrast, the high P/E's seem to have systematically earned returns *less* than that implied by their levels of risk. . . . Furthermore, the investment performance of the lowest price-earnings portfolios was also superior to that of market-based buy-and-hold portfolios, in that excess risk-adjusted returns, net of costs, could have been earned by any of three classes of investors [tax-exempt (portfolio) reallocators with zero portfolio-related costs such as colleges, tax-paying reallocators with positive costs, and speculator/traders]. . . . These *net* abnormal returns range from about 15 percent per annum to 4.5 percent per annum in magnitude depending upon the type of investor, his investment horizon and the frequency of trading" [pp. 149-50].

On the basis of this extensive and complete study which considers both risk and cost, Basu concludes that his results strongly suggest violations in the efficient markets expected-returns model. The market's reaction to price-earnings ratio information during 1957-71 was neither necessarily unbiased nor was the corrective action necessarily timely.

Two qualifications are worth mentioning. First, in one test Basu did not find significantly superior performance for the speculator/trader investor group. Second, the tax deferral advantage over his fourteen-year investment period from a buy-and-hold strategy has not been considered

---

[8] Suppose earnings information became public information sometime after the reporting date, but the period for measuring abnormal returns begins with the reporting date for statistical testing. It would then appear, erroneously, that abnormal returns could be earned.

in the net advantage calculation. Basu, as others, accepts the capital asset pricing model as a basis for his research.

Using the SEC's *Official Summary of Stock Reports,* a listing of insider transactions, Lorie and Niederhoffer [1968] found that prompt analysis of data on insider trading, published in the *Official Summary,* can be profitable, although nearly all previous published studies reached the contrary conclusion. More importantly for our purposes, the authors found (using a sample of NYSE companies during 1963 and 1964) not only that insiders usually anticipated the correct price movements of their firm's stock with their transactions, but that any investor who might have used the information on insider transactions as soon as it became publicly available would have done almost as well as the insiders. The authors attribute their results, which contradict previous studies, to better data and testing procedures. Their findings were replicated, using a much larger sample, by Pratt and De Vere [1968]. The fact that investors might profit from information on insider trading, even given the lag in its publication, has not typically been recognized.[9] Unfortunately, risk adjustments to the data were not made. In a still more recent study, Jaffe's results [1974, p. 428] "indicate that the *Official Summary* contains information on future stock prices, a finding inconsistent with much of the research on efficient capital markets." Jaffe's study did adjust for both risk and transactions costs.

3-3. EXISTENCE OF SUPERIOR TRADING
STRATEGIES: (CONDITION THREE)

Several of the studies discussed so far suggest, if they are valid despite their limitations, trading strategies which could produce excess returns. The studies described in this section deal explicitly with such trading strategies.

Breen and Savage [1968] calculated the mean return for one thousand ten-stock portfolios selected from the COMPUSTAT population and held for one year. The authors addressed several issues but only one is relevant to the issues discussed here. They examined the results of several simple portfolio selection procedures relative to random selection.

Using the computed distributions, the authors tested three reasonable and easy-to-compute portfolio selection rules against random selection. The rules involve a growth rate screen coupled with a low PE ratio (Rule 1), highest dividend return (Rule 2), and highest return on total

---

[9] See, for example, Gonedes [1972].

assets (Rule 3). After several statistical tests from using Rule 1, the authors concluded [p. 814] that their results "strongly suggest that there is a systematic component to this particular selection technique." Portfolio performance over time using Rule 1 exceeded that of randomly selected portfolios 95 per cent of the time in 10 of the 13 years examined, and the probability that this return sequence could occur by chance is one in 40 million.

Unfortunately, no corrections were made for risk (although the authors discuss the issue) or for search and transactions costs.[10] Moreover, we note that (1) the authors assumed earnings data were available on the reporting date and (2) no sensitivity analysis with respect to the length of the holding period was made. Hence we must remain skeptical of the results of this study.

In a related study with similar problems Breen [1968] again examined the performance of low price-earnings portfolios. Using the same portfolio-selection rules, he found [p. 127] that the "low price-earnings multiples, measured either relative to the whole population, or to industry classification, when combined with a control on average past growth in earnings, give portfolio performance which in most years is superior to the performance of randomly selected securities."

Once again, no corrections have been made for risk (although the authors discuss the issue) or for search and transactions costs.

In a related study McKibben [1972] uses historical accounting data in an ordinary least-squares regression model to select optimal investment portfolios. He then compares the actual return on the selected portfolios with the returns from random selection.

The variables used by McKibben include rate of return, change in earnings, growth relative to the price earnings ratio, and payout. His selected portfolios (rebalanced each year) contain twenty-eight securities and average a 29.5 percent return over the eight years of the study compared to a 16.5 percent return for the population, a difference greater than two standard deviations.

McKibben concludes [p. 371], "Although explanatory power is slight, the model selects consistently superior groups of investments, using only accounting data drawn from earlier periods. Results suggest clearly that the stock market does not follow a 'strong martingale' in which all available past information is impounded in current price." [11] McKibben also observes that his selection process does better even when

---

10 One comparison involving mutual fund data does include a two percent adjustment for transaction costs, but this adjustment is to data not used to reach the conclusions described here.

11 For the implications of a martingale, see footnote 1 to this chapter.

it is used as much as a year after the reporting date. This is potentially negative evidence to the semi-strong form of the EMH.[12]

McKibben [p. 376] comments on the problems of risk adjustment and transaction costs. He argues that, "Clearly the extra profit above the mean is large enough to cover transaction costs and still widely outperform a buy-and-hold strategy." The extra profit would also need to be adequate to cover both the costs of operationalizing his model and the associated search costs.

A potentially more serious problem concerns the issue of risk. It can be calculated, assuming the conventional Sharp-Lintner model, that the return obtained by McKibben is consistent with a portfolio beta before search and transaction costs of about 1.8.[13] Although he makes no specific adjustments for risk, he notes [p. 376] that the "sample variance for selected deciles [deciles are used to select portfolios] is *not markedly* [emphasis added] out of line with that of the population," an expected result which adds little to his case. No adjustment for search cost is included.

These comments on risk suggest an increase in risk with return. If we include the additional transaction and search costs of this method[14] and compare it with a buy-and-hold strategy, it is not clear whether the superiority of the risk-adjusted McKibben return will remain significantly better than a buy-and-hold strategy.[15, 16]

If the McKibben strategy were to yield net returns which exceeded

---

[12] It should be noted that no theory is presented to justify McKibben's model. Furthermore, the author constructs the scale-free variables by subtracting the mean return, which he then uses as a surrogate for the market return, for all stocks. This procedure assumes that the market has an identical effect on all stocks or, in other words, all securities have a beta of one.

[13] In the capital asset pricing model where $r_P = r_{ft} + \beta_p (r_{mt} - r_{ft})$, $\beta_p = \dfrac{r_{pt} - r_{ft}}{r_{mt} - r_{ft}}$ and the appropriate beta value for the McKibben portfolio depends on the assumption made about r_{ft}. Also the reported returns represent an average over eight years. Hence, the actual beta in any given year could be substantively different. The fact that only eight years are used can be expected to leave substantial variability (residual error) in the estimated beta as well.

[14] These costs could have been estimated for the straightforward approach taken.

[15] The point may be stronger since the results referenced above are based on McKibben's treatment of data as being available on the reporting date. When some delay for publication is assumed, McKibben describes his results as "weaker but still highly significant." It is not as yet obvious which is the better date to use. In defense of the earlier date, we note that it prevents any knowledge related to the first quarter's operations from influencing the results.

[16] One curiosity about the McKibben paper concerns the fact that his results are reported for only a part of the data base. The disposition (or results) of a second sample (the 280 "even" firms) created by the author is never referenced.

the market in both good and bad years then the risk issue is of no import. It is not clear that this is true for his study. McKibben presents results which compare the return on his "best" group with his population (not the market) of 280 firms for the eight years 1960-1967. While his average annual return is 29.5 percent for the best group versus an annual return of 16.5 percent on his population, the best group shows a lower return in the year 1960. On the other hand, his best group outperformed his population in 1962 and 1966, both years when his population annual return was negative. The period used in his tests is not ideal nor are his results conclusive, but they do mitigate the risk issues raised earlier.

A recent study by Jones and Litzenberger [1970] hypothesizes that reported quarterly earnings significantly greater than anticipated by market professionals from historical earnings trends would cause gradual price adjustments over time in the respective common stocks. The authors found [p. 145] that "the average price relatives of the stocks selected (those with quarterly earnings exceeding their projected quarterly earnings by at least 1.5 standard errors) in each period exceed the price relatives for Standard and Poor's Index in all ten of the periods examined." (A nonparametric sign test gave significance at the .01 level.) They conclude [p. 147] that "the market may not adjust instantaneously and correctly for every item of information that becomes available." This suggests evidence contrary to condition four as well as three. Information available to the public in the form of quarterly earnings reports does not seem to be fully discounted by the market at the time it becomes available. "If it were, stock selection techniques based on available quarterly earnings reports should not produce, on the average and over time, results significantly different from the market" [p. 147].

The study is not a complete test since the authors do not show that the profits from the trading rule used exceed the cost of information processing and transactions. "A computer is necessary to examine large quantities of data in any reasonable period of time," and "although a small investor could use similar techniques on a more limited scale," the effectiveness of the latter approach has not been researched [p. 148]. Furthermore, the data were not adjusted for risk.

Jones [1973] has extended his earlier study with Litzenberger on the use of quarterly earnings reports together with filter rules to develop trading rules that yield superior returns. Jones [p. 79] argues that, "the stock market does not discount the information content of favorable quarterly earning reports instantaneously. . . . [I]ncreased professional interest caused by the favorable earnings report is gradually disseminated to the general investing public through brokers and advisory services.

The consequent increase in demand for the security would be expected to generate a trend in the price of stock." [17]

Jones uses a computerized earnings-trend model to isolate stocks whose earnings significantly exceed their trend. Jones notes that the stocks selected consistently outperformed the market, and by substantial amounts in some periods.

Jones does not adjust for the costs of his approach, but he does address the question of risk. We note that adjusting for search and transaction costs in this model is more difficult than, say, with the McKibben approach. In the Jones study, search costs are a random variable since they are based on a probabilistic filter rule. For example, using Jones' model there is no guarantee that any investments would be signaled in a given period, particularly for small investors operating on a more limited scale.

Although the stocks selected by the Jones earnings-trend model show [pp. 81-82] "a higher systematic risk (proportionate rate responsiveness greater than unity), their mean realized rate of return on a risk-adjusted basis was still quite superior to that of the Standard and Poor's Industrial Index." [18] This study by Jones uses data over the period 1965 to mid-1969. During this time the market experienced a substantial rise. It would have been interesting if Jones had been able to carry his study ahead a couple of years. The behavior of his model and the associated costs we suspect would be less favorable in a period characterized by a falling (or more volatile) market.

Homa and Jaffee [1971] describe a model which enables them to predict the Standard and Poor's 500 stock index on a quarterly basis using the supply of money and its growth rate as independent variables. Then, by using the predicted S & P values, they are able to simulate investors' decisions as to investments in Treasury bills, common stock, and margined common stock. The value of the information obtained from the Standard and Poor's index prediction depended on the investors' ability to forecast the money supply. When the money supply is predicted using the unemployment rate, the rate of inflation, and a variable related to the U.S. international reserve position as independent variables in a regression equation, the simulations showed that investors would earn higher rates of return than could be achieved by a simply buy-and-hold strategy, even after adjusting for transactions costs. Furthermore, the standard deviation of the returns was actually reduced.

---

[17] The approach relies on the work of Cootner [1962].

[18] It is possible that the beta based on past data might underestimate the current beta, given that the stocks selected had earnings significantly in excess of their trend.

The use of margins and the ability to predict the money supply with perfect accuracy, of course, caused the excess rate of return to be even larger, but the standard deviation of the returns increased when margins were introduced. Costs of operationalizing the model, if small, might be reasonably omitted.

Malkiel and Quandt [1972] are critical of the Homa and Jaffee model since they [p. 926] "found that the Homa and Jaffee model no longer performed better than the naive investment strategy when the time period was extended to include 1970 and when revised measures of the money supply were employed." Malkiel and Quandt offer an alternative model based on fiscal rather than monetary variables. Their model consistently outperforms the buy-and-hold strategy and the Homa and Jaffee model. However, Malkiel and Quandt are quick to provide some caveats in considering their results. Their model is sensitive to the time period involved and to small changes in the definitions of the variables. Thus prediction accuracy in the past may not continue in the future. Also, their model has no provisions for identifying structural changes in the economy and usually fails to forecast important turning points.[19]

A recent study by Zweig [1973] provides further evidence in conflict with the EMH by suggesting how investor expectations can be used to develop profitable trading rules using publicly available information.[20]

Zweig develops his trading model using the premiums on closed-end mutual funds. The logic behind his approach is illustrated by the following quote [p. 68]: "for example, assume non-professionals are active in the market for closed-end funds, but that these vehicles do not appeal to the professional. When the non-professionals in general become extremely bullish, they bid up prices of all stocks, including closed-end fund shares. The professionals realizing that stocks have become overvalued, enter the market as sellers, thereby tending to bring stock prices down. However, they fail to enter the closed-end fund market. Thus, while the net asset values of closed-end funds are subject to activities of both professionals and nonprofessionals, the share prices of the funds themselves are affected only by the behavior of the non-professionals. Hence, the differential between net asset values and closed-end fund share prices (the premium or discount) can be used to identify the expectations of the non-professionals."

Zweig develops a trading rule which produces buy (sell) signals when the proportion of negative (positive) premium changes exceed a

---

[19] Forecasting turning points for the return series of individual stocks suggests a possible means of testing the EMH using a nonlinear approach.

[20] His approach, like that of Jones, finds its roots in Cootner [1962].

trigger set by a given filter rule. Using his optimal filter rule and making allowances for transaction costs, Zweig's trading rule produces a return significantly larger (at the .05 probability level) than that obtained using a buy-and-hold strategy.[21]

No allowance was made for risk since Zweig is concerned with the buying and selling of fund (or portfolio) shares with betas that might be expected to be nearly equal to one. Thus, this is a less serious problem than in studies with similar objectives that failed to make risk adjustments. Nevertheless, such adjustments should have been made since most portfolios do not have betas precisely equal to one.

Grier and Albin [1973] study large block trades on the NYSE and find a strong tendency for price changes just prior to these trades to be in the opposite direction from price changes just after the trades. They present a filter trading rule that is based upon this tendency. They rank a large sample of block trades with respect to the change between the opening price on the day of the transaction and the price at which the block traded. For the five percent of the trades for which these changes had the largest negative values, the filter rule dictates purchase of the stock at the price at which the block traded and sale at the closing price for the day. Had this rule been followed with a sample of 200 blocks that were traded during the last quarter of 1968 and the first quarter of 1969, it would have resulted in an annualized return, after allowing for transaction costs of 2% per trade, of more than 1000%.

Reback [1974] is highly critical of the Grier and Albin results on several grounds. First, investors are usually not able to buy a stock at the price at which a block of that stock was traded. Grier and Albin attempted to compensate for this problem by performing a test of their filter trading rule using as the purchase price the price of a transaction occurring 15 minutes after the block. They state that there is no significant change in their results using this later price. Reback also argues that the 2% transaction cost used by Grier and Albin is too low and that a more realistic cost would eliminate their findings of substantial excess returns. Nevertheless, since floor traders and specialists are able to avoid some of the transaction costs, the opportunity for excess returns appears to be available to at least some of the market participants.

Another problem with the Grier and Albin study is the reporting

---

[21] His procedure produces better results over all fifteen filter percentages examined. Further, his model produces more trade signals than could be attributed to chance ($a = .05$), and, according to Zweig, it demonstrates a market tendency for signals at all filter levels to accurately forecast the one-week direction of Dow Jones price movements.

of an annualized rate of return when the actual trading rule involves transactions occurring within single trading days. On many trading days no block trades that meet the filter rule's requirements take place, while on other days several may occur. However, someone using this trading rule must keep the necessary amount of capital readily available to react immediately to each new block trade. Thus, the annual excess return of 1000% appears to be unrealistically high. Furthermore, as Kraus and Stoll [1972] show in a study discussed in Chapter 2, there is no predictable price behavior after the day on which the block trade occurred.

3-4. INSTANTANEOUS AND UNBIASED RESPONSE: (CONDITION FOUR)

That lags in market adjustment do exist has been documented. One of the more celebrated instances occurred in 1968 when information concerning significantly lower quarterly earnings for Control Data was made known at the annual stockholder's meeting. The stock held for two days but then dropped $16.75 (11 percent in one day on a volume of 900,000 shares, nearly two-thirds of this volume being accounted for by six blocks (each in excess of 19,000 shares).[22]

It is worth noting that this instance (or even similar ones) does not necessarily violate the EMH. If the expected value of the new information available at stockholder meetings is, as might be anticipated, low, then this case can be attributed to rational behavior on the part of analysts concerned with the costs of obtaining information. The fact that one knew later that this would have been a useful meeting to attend is irrelevant.

Kaplan and Roll [1972] study the effect of accounting alternatives on the investment credit and the depreciation switchback on annual price changes. Their results, subject to a recognized preselection bias, suggest [p. 245] that "relying strictly on averages, however, one can conclude that security prices increase around the date when a firm announces earnings inflated by an accounting change." They go on to observe [p. 245] that "the effect appears to be temporary, and, certainly by the subsequent quarterly report, the price has resumed a level appropriate to the true economic status of the firm."

Although there appears to be some anticipation by the market, the possibility of abnormal returns seems to exist given the figures reported

---

[22] Reported in Smidt [1968]. He also makes the point described in the next paragraph.

by Kaplan and Roll. The study suggests possible short-run inefficiencies in the market and it is unfortunate that the authors did not comment on this implication of their study. Furthermore, the use of averages may mask individual effects.

A recent study by Ball [1972] finds evidence contrary to that in Kaplan and Roll's work. Ball suggests that information on changes in accounting methods may yield information about the systematic risk characteristics of the firm. Arguing that the systematic risk characteristics of a stock may change, Ball shows that Kaplan and Roll's assumption of stationarity can lead to a misestimation of the expected returns. Ball finds that his data with respect to changes in accounting are consistent with the EMH once adjustments for the changing risk characteristic have been made. We shall have more to say about this study in the next chapter.

3-5. CONCLUSIONS

The studies cited represent only a small portion of the total research on the EMH. Nevertheless they raise questions about the descriptive validity of the hypothesis, in its semi-strong form. On the other hand, most of these studies can be criticized for a failure to adjust for the market (that is, work with residuals or, in other words, control for the systematic risk). Some of the studies also fail to adjust for transactions and search costs. Hence, we cannot simply accept their results at face value. Indeed, the research cited seems to be, in general, of poorer quality than that supporting the model. Nevertheless, the issues raised are important and should not be ignored. We believe more research is required before the issues can be resolved.

As a practical matter, we also wonder about the impact of the EMH on the investment community. The implication of the hypothesis in its weak and semi-strong form is toward some diminution in the size and impact of this economic activity or at least a change in emphasis on evaluation techniques such as charting. We wonder what an empirical study of these issues would show.

The EMH, like any other extreme null hypothesis, is not likely to be literally true. If systematic tendencies do exist, then it behooves researchers to attempt to discover their size and extent as well as the implications for the market. It is a question of learning more about the market frictions that cause perturbations in the predictions of the model. Smidt [1968] suggests three sources of such systematic behavior: the demand for liquidity, lags in response to new information, and inappropriate information response.[23]

We should, then, not be surprised if we find some evidence of systematic dependencies in price changes. But, the profits available from exploiting such dependencies should, if the EMH holds, be at most those necessary to attract and hold resources in the activity of eliminating them. Results by Fama [1965A] and by Fama and Blume [1966] appear to confirm this. Tests which identify specific alternative hypotheses that seem to be most likely on an a priori basis are more powerful than those that do not do so.[24]

3-6. SUMMARY

In this chapter we have attempted to add to the discussion of efficient markets as it has appeared in the accounting literature. In particular, we have surveyed several studies not often referenced which question the frictionless nature of the hypothesis as it is usually described.

In the next chapter, we examine several problems associated with the models used in testing for efficient markets. Again the reader is urged to view the available evidence as related to the degree of efficiency in the market.

[23] Some work has already been done here. See, for example, Niederhoffer and Osborne [1966]. They deal with the liquidity issue but the study can be considered as a test of the strong form of the EMH.

[24] Such tests would be more powerful than the simple null-hypothesis test. See Smidt [1968].

CHAPTER FOUR

Evidence on the Adequacy of the Economic Models and Assumptions

The purpose of this chapter is to examine some of the assumptions of the models used to conduct research on efficient markets. The issues raised here do not question the Efficient Market Hypothesis (EMH) directly; rather, they involve the factors that make adequate testing more difficult.

The EMH is a statement about the expectation of security returns given certain types of information. The hypothesis thus requires some theory which allows this expectation of security returns to be estimated. For this purpose, researchers have used the theory of capital asset pricing and the related market model of portfolio selection.

The EMH is a statement about expectations. But if the hypothesis is to be a reasonably accurate description of security returns, then securities must be (approximately) properly priced relative to one another. A theory is needed, then, to specify the appropriate relationships between the individual stocks' expected returns and hence to establish the specific stock prices. One such theory that has gained substantial support and which was discussed earlier is expressed in the Capital Asset Pricing Model (CAPM) developed by Sharpe [1964], Lintner [1965B], and Mossin [1966].

Since the CAPM is expressed in terms of expectations which are unobservable, tests of the EMH have usually been based on a theory about the market process which generates security prices. This theory is expressed operationally by the market model developed by Markowitz [1952] and Sharpe [1963]. Both the CAPM and the market model allow the researcher to estimate a series of excess returns which can be related to the information series resulting from accounting reports.[1] A number of studies using this approach are discussed in Chapters 2 and 3. Yet, if the supportive research described in Chapter 2 is to be accepted, the assumptions underlying the model used to obtain the excess return series must be reasonably accurate. (The same point holds for Chapter 3.)

The assumptions required by the CAPM and market model are described in some detail in Appendix B. In this chapter we will discuss only those assumptions which have been seriously questioned by empirical investigation. Lengthy consideration will not be given those assumptions which, although of questionable face validity, have been shown by empirical research either to have a limited effect or to be reasonably approximated by the models. The assumptions discussed here are:

4-1. Assumption One: Existence of a Risk-Free Asset: Investors can borrow or lend unlimited amounts at a common and exogeneously determined riskless rate.

4-2. Assumption Two: The Two Parameter Model: Investors select among securities using the expectation and variability (where variability is measured by the variance) of returns.

4-3. Assumption Three: Risk Avoidance: Investors wish to avoid risk. They are risk averse. (This implies that greater risk will be accepted by investors only if expected returns are larger.)

4-4. Assumption Four: No Industry Effects: The return on a security is a function of a single variable (the security's systematic risk) which measures the covariance of the security's return with the market. No industry effect is included in the model.

4-5. Assumption Five: Homogeneous Expectations: Investors possess identical expectations about the mean return and its variability with all assets.[2]

---

[1] It may, however, not be adequate merely to estimate the excess returns without determining the reasons for them. Excess returns may be due to chance or to events unrelated to accounting reports.

[2] See Appendix A for a discussion of means, variances, and covariances.

4-1. EXISTENCE OF A RISK-FREE ASSET: (ASSUMPTION ONE)

The main result of the CAPM is a statement to the effect that an asset's expected excess return is directly proportional to its systematic risk as measured by the asset's beta. This implies a linear relationship between an asset's expected return and its beta. As is shown in Appendix B, equation (B3), the constant term in this linear relationship can be written as the return on a riskless asset.

Black, Jensen, and Scholes [1972] conducted extensive time-series regression tests of the validity of this model. Their results suggest that the model fails to provide an accurate description of the structure of security returns. The results show returns on low beta assets to be higher than expected.

In other words, an asset's expected excess return is not strictly proportional to its beta and vice versa for high beta stocks. The results confirm the cross-sectional findings made by Miller and Scholes [1972].

If the assumption of riskless borrowing and lending is relaxed, Black, Jensen, and Scholes find that the expected returns of an asset are better explained by a two-parameter model involving the assets's beta and the return on an asset that has a zero covariance, a zero beta, with the return on the market portfolio. [In equation (B3), it is the return on this zero-beta asset that replaces the r_{ft} factor.] Black [1972] has shown that such a model is appropriate when riskless borrowing opportunities are not available.

Blume and Friend [1973] examine the unlimited borrowing assumption under the condition of a perfectly functioning short-selling mechanism. (This condition appears slightly more restrictive than that of a risk-free rate but it may not cause problems for capital asset pricing theory, according to the authors, if it so happened that each investor's optimal portfolio involved no negative or short holdings. In this case an investor's portfolio could be considered as a linear combination of the market portfolio and a portfolio with a zero beta.[3] Such a zero-beta

---

[3] The theory behind the model which explains security returns as a linear combination of the market portfolio and an efficient zero-beta portfolio is contained in Black [1972]. It is worth observing that the theory is not entirely free of criticisms. In a comment on Black's paper, Stone [1972] asserts that:

Black omits the imposition of any market clearing requirements which, when added, lead to restrictions on the weights of Black's basic portfolios. This in turn implies one is not free (as Black assumes) to choose both the market portfolio and a zero-beta portfolio as basic portfolios.

portfolio might necessitate short sales if it were actually held. But if no short sales were made because there were no short positions required, the short-sale condition would be less restrictive.)

Blume and Friend [p. 30] conclude that, "The evidence . . . seems to require rejection of the capital assets pricing theory as an explanation of the observed returns on *all* [emphasis added] financial assets. . . . This theory implies untenable estimates of the rates of return on assets which are risk free or virtually so." [4]

However, Blume and Friend [p. 26] also find that, "a linear model is a tenable approximation of the empirical relationship between return and risk for NYSE stocks over the period [1955-1968] covered." If the market for what the authors call "well-seasoned" common stocks is at least partially segmented from the markets for other assets (such as bonds), then the CAPM with the short-sale assumptions may still be useful in explaining returns in the more restricted market.[5]

It can be asserted that questions concerning the risk-free rate are of minimal importance given the way these models are used, at least for the research done in accounting. The assertion is that the resolution of the issues surrounding the risk-free rate makes no difference to the empirical results. But we cannot be sure of this. The CAPM and market model are the theoretical justification for the empirical steps undertaken by the researcher. If this theory is not sufficient, then the basis of our empirical work is eroded and the research results questionable. Until a more promising theory is presented and validated, we cannot be sure that employing it in empirical research in accounting will not yield substantive dif-

---

In a subsequent paper, Stone [1973, p. 1] shows that the appropriate interpretation of the intercept term is simply a certainty-equivalent rate and not the return on an *inefficient* minimum-variance zero-beta portfolio. He further criticizes the idea that all efficient portfolios are a linear combination of the market and a zero-beta portfolio by showing that such an assumption implies both different certainty-equivalent rates and different rates of substitution of return for standard deviation at every risk level, a property which Stone argues is not compatible with usual concepts of market equilibrium.

Several writers (including Stone) also argue that Black, Jensen, and Scholes [1972] obtained results consistent with Black's model because the construction of their test made it a test merely of a regression identity. See Fama and MacBeth [1973], and Sunder [1973].

[4] The statement is conditional on the return generating process for common stocks taking the form

$$\tilde{r}_i = E(\tilde{r}_i) + \tilde{\delta}_1 + \beta_i(\tilde{\delta}_2 - \tilde{\delta}_1) + \tilde{\epsilon}_i$$

where $\tilde{r}_i$ is the return on asset i, $\tilde{\delta}_1$ and $\tilde{\delta}_2$ are two factors common to all securities. The tilde signifies a random variable.

[5] It is also important to note the relevance of this finding to the existence of nonlinear dependencies on which superior trading strategies might be built. The expected-returns model denies the existence of such profitable trading rules.

ferences. An example of a proposed alternate theory with some intuitive appeal is provided by the Kraus and Litzenberger model discussed in the next section.

The most extensive tests to date of the CAPM were conducted by Fama and MacBeth [1973]. They used a linear regression equation involving the following three independent variables to explain portfolio returns: (1) the average of the systematic risk coefficients calculated for each security from the one-factor market model, a portfolio beta, (2) the average of the square of this systematic risk coefficient for all of the individual securities in the portfolio, and (3) the average standard deviation of the least squares residuals from the one-factor market model for each security. They tested their regression model on twenty NYSE portfolios over the period January 1935 through June 1968. Subperiods were also examined. The portfolios were constructed using ranked values of the systematic risk coefficients with appropriate precautions taken to minimize measurement errors.

The testable hypotheses were formulated as follows:

1. The relationship between the expected return on a security and its risk in any efficient portfolio is linear.
2. The systematic risk coefficient is a complete measure of the risk of a security in the efficient portfolio.
3. Higher risk should be associated with higher return.
4. The two parameter model holds.[6]

(The first two hypotheses imply that the regression coefficients of the second and third independent variables are each expected to be zero. The third hypothesis suggests that the expected value of the coefficient of the first independent variable is the expected return on the market portfolio in excess of the return on the riskless asset. And the fourth hypothesis suggests that the expected value of the constant term in the regression equation is the return on a riskless asset.) Because of the care and completeness of this study, we report at this point briefly on all of the hypotheses tested despite the fact that only the fourth specifically relates to the risk-free rate issue.

Fama and MacBeth conclude by arguing that [p. 633], "we cannot reject the hypothesis that average returns on New York Stock Exchange common stocks reflect efficient portfolios. Specifically, on average there

[6] This is the traditional

$$\tilde{r}_{pt} = r_{ft} + \beta_p (\tilde{r}_{mt} - r_{ft})$$

CAPM which assumes unrestricted riskless borrowing and lending at the rate r_{ft}.

seems to be a positive tradeoff between return and risk, with risk measured from the portfolio viewpoint. In addition, although there are 'stochastic nonlinearities' from period-to-period, we cannot reject the hypothesis that on average their effects are zero and unpredictably different from zero from one period to the next. Thus, we cannot reject the hypothesis that in making a portfolio decision, an investor should assume that the relationship between a security's portfolio risk and its expected return is linear, as implied by the two parameter model. We also cannot reject the hypothesis of the two-parameter model that no measure of risk, in addition to portfolio risks, systematically affects average returns."

Thus, they are not able to reject the first three hypotheses. However, their tests of the fourth hypothesis were ambiguous. In most of the periods tested, the two parameter model was inadequate: the constant term was significantly greater than the return on a risk-free asset. This finding is not surprising and is consistent with the conclusions of Blume and Friend [1973] and Black, Jensen, and Scholes [1972]. However, there is sufficient ambiguity in the data and tests to cause one to be cautious in accepting the confirmation of the results just cited. Moreover, reading successive drafts of the paper suggests the authors found it a difficult task to draw final conclusions concerning their results and those of previous researchers about the risk-free rate.[7]

Brenner [1974B] has assessed the importance of the correct specification of the market model in conducting empirical tests of capital market efficiency. Using the methodology developed by Fama, Fisher, Jensen, and Roll [1969], Brenner tests the sensitivity of the results concerning the efficiency of the market in reacting to information for five forms of the market model, including the form based on the existence of the risk-free asset and the form based on the zero-beta asset. He finds relatively minor differences among the results using the different models and argues that the decision about whether tests of market efficiency are sensitive to the form of the market model depends on how these results are inter-

---

[7] Brenner [1974A] offers an interesting extension of the Fama and MacBeth tests. If Black's zero-beta model is valid, the average value of β_o should be zero, i.e.,

$$\beta_o = \frac{cov(\tilde{r}_o'\tilde{r}_m)}{\sigma^2(\tilde{r}_m)} = 0$$

where $\tilde{r}_o' \equiv$ return on a portfolio whose return is uncorrelated with the market return,
   $\tilde{r}_m \equiv$ return on the market,
   $\sigma^2(\tilde{r}_m) \equiv$ variance of the return on the market.

Using regression estimates from Fama and MacBeth, Brenner finds that β_o is always greater than zero (and usually significantly so) for the entire period as well as for the sub-periods tested by Fama and MacBeth. This evidence favors the original two parameter model and casts additional doubt on Black's zero-beta model.

preted. He concludes his study by recommending that future tests of market efficiency be conducted using more than one form of the market model.

These issues lead us naturally to some discussion of the two parameter model.

4-2. THE TWO PARAMETER MODEL: (ASSUMPTION TWO)

The EMH has its mathematical expression in the expected-returns model (see Appendix B). This model operationalizes the notion that an investor cannot use publicly available information to increase his own utility where utility is defined only in terms of expected returns. Yet utility is certainly not likely to be a single-dimensional concept. Financial statements provide information on risk as well and, as we saw in Chapter 1, this is an important element in the two parameter CAPM. Either or both of these two variables can produce market effects. Further, it is possible that their effects may be offsetting. This makes it more difficult to test the EMH.

The basic problem is further complicated by other sources of market disequilibria. Two such possibilities are suggested by Ball [1972]. They are the information concerning expected future returns for assets in general and information causing changes in the relative risks of stocks and their expected rates of return.

But expectations and variances may be inadequate variables with which to explain how investors select their security holdings. Arditti [1967], for one, suggests that skewness (see Appendix A) may also be relevant to evaluating performance and hence, by implication, relevant to investment selection as well.

He includes a measure of skewness, along with the variance and the market correlation coefficient, in a cross-sectional regression and finds it to be significant in explaining security returns. In a still more recent article, Arditti [1971] finds that both the realized market returns and the returns for a sample of thirty-four mutual funds are positively skewed, with the funds having a greater amount of positive skewness. He concludes [p. 912], "The implication is that fund managers are willing to give up some expected return or to take on a bit more variability in exchange for a greater chance at a large annual return."

In an effort to determine the impact of positive skewness on the results obtained from empirical tests of the CAPM, Miller and Scholes

[1972] simulate the effects on beta and the residual variance of positively skewed returns for a sample of six hundred "companies." They find that the introduction of skewness causes the estimated security beta to overstate the true beta and the estimated residual variance to understate the true residual variance.

These results can be interpreted as implying a need either for more rigorous testing of the extant theory or for a major modification to the theory. Kraus and Litzenberger [1972] have provided the latter by adding a measure of systematic skewness to the traditional CAPM model. They test their model on twenty portfolios of NYSE stocks over a 32-year period and find that the measure of systematic skewness is a statistically significant explanatory factor of security returns. The modification suggested to the CAPM makes the expected return on a security a function of systematic skewness as well as of systematic risk.

Previous tests of the traditional CAPM using a cross-sectional analysis [8] found that estimates of the constant term which represents the return on a risk-free asset are significantly greater than zero and that estimates of the slope are positive but only about half as large as the mean excess rate of return on the market index. When Kraus and Litzenberger add their systematic measure of portfolio skewness as a second explanatory variable, they find that the estimate of the intercept is not significantly different from zero, the estimate of the market price of beta is significantly positive and larger than the estimates from the traditional model, and the estimate of the market price of skewness is significantly negative, which is consistent with the theory since the market index was positively skewed over the test period. Furthermore, the sum of the two-slope coefficients is not significantly different from the mean excess rate of return on the market index. The authors conclude [p. 18] that their study "suggests that the prior negative empirical findings . . . that were attributed to restrictions on riskless borrowing resulted instead from misspecification of the CAPM by the omission of systematic skewness." The importance of the specification error to results from accounting research has not yet been evaluated by empirical studies. It could, for example, explain the results obtained by Basu [1974] reported in Chapter 3.

Still another aspect of the two parameter model involves the relationship between a stock's return and the variance of the stock's return. Using a regression model Douglas [1969] related returns for a large cross-section sample of common stocks to their own variance and to a market-index covariance term constructed from the sample. His results showed a significant and positive relation to the security's own variance but not

[8] See Friend and Blume [1970]; Black, Jensen, and Scholes [1972]; and Fama and MacBeth [1973].

to the market-index covariance. But under the CAPM, the coefficient of the stock's own variance term should be zero.

Douglas also discussed some unpublished work by Lintner that yielded a nonzero coefficient for the variance of the residuals from the time-series regression line, when this was used as an additional variable. The coefficient of this variance variable in Lintner's work was positive and as significant as the coefficient of the market term.

Miller and Scholes [1972] ran exhaustive tests on the measurement and other assumptions that might have accounted for the Douglas-Lintner results. Miller and Scholes suggest that the combined effects of skewness in the returns distributions with random measurement errors in the market-index covariance parameter could, in principle, produce the Douglas-Lintner results. Jensen [1972], however, does not believe the Miller-Scholes tests will explain the results he obtained with Black and Scholes [1972], and to which we referred earlier. It would seem the answers are not yet firm on tests of the type described here.

4-3. RISK AVOIDANCE: (ASSUMPTION THREE)

Jacob's [1971] empirical study of the CAPM addresses the observed consistency among average return and systematic risk measures (implied by the risk-avoidance assumption) during single time periods and the extent to which these relationships are maintained in succeeding periods. She concludes [p. 832] that, "an investor is likely to find that the average return on his portfolio will not, in general, be highly consistent with its degree of systematic risk." Neither of Jacob's measures of systematic risk provide sufficient information on return. Other factors such as (1) length of the time horizon used to generate the holding period return distributions, (2) the market's average return over this horizon, (3) the length of the intended holding period, (4) the number of securities in the investor's portfolio, and (5) the method the investor uses to select securities, are shown by Jacob to be relevant variables.

Jacob's research suggests further that the relationships between systematic risk and average return are not stable. This introduces the problem of parameter stability to which we now address ourselves.

The assumption that investors are averse to risk means that greater risk will be accepted only if expected returns are larger. In other words, as the risk of a security increases so does the expected return: expected returns are positively correlated with risks. The generally accepted theory connecting risk and return is formally expressed by the market model in which the expected return on a security is a linear function of a market index. The coefficient of the market index is a measure of the volatility or risk of the security and is usually called the security's beta. The empirical tests of the EMH have almost without exception assumed the beta for a given security is stationary over time.[9]

Malkiel and Cragg [1970] related the ratio of market prices divided by earnings to earnings growth, dividend payout, expectations of long-term earnings growth, measures of normal earning power, and estimates of instability. Although an extremely close fit to the empirical structures of share prices was obtained, the coefficients of the equation change considerably (and significantly at the .0001 level) from year to year and in a manner that is consistent with the changing standards of value in vogue at the time. In other words, individuals in the aggregate, experience changes in their investment attitudes toward the variables included in this study. Indeed if the general desire for earnings growth changes from time to time, then there is no reason to expect the beta coefficients to be stationary over time.

Blume [1971] studied the time stability of the beta coefficients for both single stocks and portfolios of several sizes, using correlation techniques. His assessment procedures compare the correlations of the portfolio betas for consecutive seven-year periods where the portfolios are constructed of stocks with consecutive beta values in the initial periods.

For single-stock portfolios, the correlations were about 0.60 while for ten-stock portfolios the correlations were around 0.90. Blume also found some mean-regressive tendency for the individual betas; that is, when a beta departed from its average value, the expected direction of the next change was toward its average. Although his measurements of this tendency were time dependent, improved predictions were obtained using regression equations that reflected this tendency.[10]

Sharpe and Cooper [1972] have conducted an exhaustive study of individual security beta coefficients over time. By classifying the betas in each year by deciles (which they call risk-return classes), they examine beta stability by the tendency for the security betas to shift deciles. Sharpe and Cooper provide transition matrices for year t to year $t+1$ and for year t to year $t+5$. The proportion of security betas in the same risk-return class varied from 0.75 to 0.35 after one year and from 0.40 to 0.13 after five years. The proportion within one risk-return class varies from 0.93 to 0.78 after one year and from 0.69 to 0.39 after five years.

---

[9] We note that the CAPM is essentially a static equilibrium one-period model. There is no theoretical basis to assume that any of its parameters are stable over time. See Appendix B.

[10] Beaver [1970] found that accounting rates of return are also mean-regressive. The mean-regressive tendency of the betas was also found by R. Levy [1971].

Sharpe and Cooper concluded [p. 54] that "there is substantial stability over time, even at the level of individual securities." We only point out that the data are consistent with viewing the stability assumption as at best an approximation. Examination of the betas for individual stocks as reported by Sharpe and Cooper in their Table IV suggest that at least some security betas have been highly volatile.

The beta stability question was studied for time periods of less than a year by Levy [1971]. Levy also observed the tendency of the betas to be more stable for larger portfolios. His results, obtained by an approach similar to Blume's, show correlations that range from below 0.50 for single-stock portfolios to about 0.85 for ten-stock portfolios. The correlations are substantially lower for shorter time periods and this is important if these shorter periods are more relevant for security analysis.

An alternative approach used by Aber [1972] examines stability for a given security. Stability is inferred by the ability of beta values derived from different time periods, using regression techniques, to produce similar distributions of security returns when applied to identical market-index values.[11] This approach allows Aber to deal with the implicit uncertainty in the estimates of the betas as they apply to single securities. Aber concludes from his tests that a low degree of parameter stability exists.[12]

A recent study by Meyers [1973] presents further evidence that the beta values are unstable. In particular, his empirical evidence questions the assumption for the period 1950-1967. Meyers divides the time period into two parts and computes the percentages of variance in the logarithms of monthly price relatives for ninety-four stocks in both periods. The degree of stationarity in the individual betas is suggested by the stationarity of these percentages in the two periods. Meyers [p. 321] finds that "for more than one-fourth of the companies . . . the percentage of variance associated with the market factor in one period is more than twice the percentage in the other period, and the difference is more than ten percentage points for more than half the sample."[13]

Although no criterion exists by which acceptable limits for assuming stationarity can be established, Meyers [p. 321] concludes that his evidence reflects "unquestionable evidence of serious violations of the stationarity assumption . . . it appears the differences for at least a

---

[11] Aber's approach allows him to use multi-market-index models while avoiding the difficulties in analysis caused by multicollinearity. The results described here, however, are restricted to a single market-index model for consistency reasons.

[12] Also see Jacob [1971].

[13] The averages over the ninety-four companies for the two periods were, as is to be expected, almost identical.

fourth, and probably half, of the companies in the sample exceed reasonable limits."

Meyers notes further that the effect of nonstationarity on the conclusions of prior studies concerned with the information content of accounting data cannot be determined on the basis of available evidence. But, as he implies, replicating (hopefully some of the better) studies using only stocks with reasonably stationary betas over the entire period examined could provide some insights.

Several writers have developed theoretical models which have implications for the stability of beta. A brief review is useful since the implications were not always recognized by researchers.

Brennan [1973] provides a multi-period capital market equilibrium model. This model assumes individuals make decisions between consumption and investment in order to maximize expected utility. Brennan's results [p. 671], generally yield betas which are not stationary.

In another recent study LeRoy [1973] examines the conditions under which a stock's expected rate of return depends on its realized rate of return. He finds [p. 455] that if we can assume investors to be risk averse, a dependence exists between expected and realized returns. This result can be construed as suggesting a lack of stationarity in the beta coefficient under the conventional model which posits a one-to-one relationship between a stock's beta coefficient and its rate of return.

The importance of the stability of the individual betas declines, as we have seen, for larger portfolios since their relevance to portfolio risk is their contribution to the average squared portfolio beta.[14] It may be possible even in high- (low-) risk strategy portfolios to eliminate through diversification most of the effect of shifting beta values for individual securities held. Also, for portfolios of relatively small size which involve a moderate risk strategy, movements of individual betas will tend to offset one another.

These facts do not mitigate, however, the importance of stability for those investors with either small or risk-similar holdings or for those who do not (by choice) hold well-diversified portfolios. In these cases, changes in the beta values can lead to transactions costs. This is particularly likely to be the case for high- (or low-) risk strategies.

The stability question is doubly important for another reason. The question of the information content of accounting reports is considered by adjusting individual stock returns for the market effect using

---

[14] Evans and Archer [1968] have shown empirically that most of the diversification effect relative to individual security risk can be obtained with ten or more securities.

that stock's beta. Thus, this information is stock specific. If stability only holds for portfolios, then the difficulties in evaluating the information content of accounting reports is more complex than is suggested by most of the existing research.

Logic as well as the empirical results tells us to expect changes in these coefficients due to such events as changes in tastes, mergers, the effect of changing economic conditions on growth firms, the effect of changes in the debt-equity ratio caused by new issues, debt retirements or shifts in the level of a stock's price, and governmental policies in the areas of trade, taxes and so on. Hamada [1969], among others has shown analytically that a firm's beta increases with leverage.[15] Brenner and Smidt [1974] develop an asset valuation theory consistent with the CAPM which predicts non-stationary beta coefficients that vary inversely with the value of the asset. Their empirical work indicates that this theory does nearly as well as assuming that the beta coefficients are stationary for NYSE-listed companies. Further, there is no reason to expect such changes to be either smooth or continuous over time. Hence, the question becomes one of estimating or predicting the appropriate beta value (or set of values) for a firm or portfolio over the selected time period of interest.

Since there is no theoretical justification in the models themselves for stationarity of the beta coefficient over time, we might ask why this assumption was implicit in much of the early empirical work. Of course, we can only speculate.

Initial authors essentially avoided the issue. We suspect that this was in part because these researchers had some doubts concerning stationarity. However, at the time no suitable theory was present to suggest how beta values might change, that is, how they might be functionally related to other fundamental economic variables. Since some assumption concerning the stability question would be implicit to any empirical work, it was considered appropriate to complete the data analysis and hope the assumption of stationarity was sufficiently accurate to yield useful results.

Furthermore, in studying the effects of accounting changes one must be careful that the changes do not reflect the impact of real economic changes on the firm. If the accounting change is associated

---

[15] Stone [1974] has shown analytically that warrant financing can be a source of systematic price dependence in a stock's beta and thus a source of beta instability. Black and Scholes [1973] in connection with the pricing of call options show that the beta coefficient of the option depends on the price of the underlying asset, and hence is not stationary. As the authors point out, the common stock of a levered company has many of the characteristics of an option.

with events of economic content and these economic events are, in turn, associated with changes in the relative risk of the firm, the beta coefficient will change.

Ball [1972] made an attempt to adjust the data for non-stationarity of the betas. Ball's study presents results consistent with the EMH after such adjustments. Such data corrections are appropriate. It is of interest to note that these corrections were not made until research yielded indications of market inefficiency.

However, Ball employed ordinary-least-squares regression estimates over a moving time series for each month. Sunder [1973] notes that since this procedure gives the same weight to all observations, it is not an efficient method for estimating risk in a changing environment.[16] However, in neither the Ball nor the Sunder studies were the adjustments based upon any hypothesized relationships between events impinging on the firm's activities and a change in its risk parameter. We do not know the impact of Ball's and Sunder's procedures on the data and hence its effect on the results of their studies. Sunder indicates he is working on a research design in which the measurement of abnormal price changes considers risk changes using techniques that can be shown to be optimal in an unstable environment. The resulting price-change estimates are adjusted for both the market factor and for changes in relative risk.

The work of Beaver, Kettler, and Scholes [1970] suggests that information on risk is a potentially important area in which accounting can be of value given that markets are efficient. They found significant associations of market-determined risk measures with accounting estimates of risk and further, that accounting risk measures could be used as instrumental variables in ways that improved on forecasts of market risk compared to forecasts based on value models using past observations. These associations are confirmed by other authors including Ball and Brown [1969], Beaver and Manegold [1973], Logue and Merville [1972], and Gonedes [1973]. Gonedes, however, found the explanatory power of the accounting-based estimates of risk to be low. We note in passing that if beta values are unstable and, hence, difficult to estimate, their use in validating these independently derived accounting risk measures is open to question.

Rosenberg and McKibben [1973] use both sources of information —fundamental accounting data and the historical distribution of returns —to predict a stock's current beta and its residual risk (that is, that part

16 Sunder cites several authors who have proposed estimation procedures which are optimal in an unstable environment.

of a stock's total variability which is uncorrelated with the market). They find [p. 331] that in predicting betas, "the additional information provided by the accounting descriptors, is small." On the other hand, they found that historical price behavior did provide additional information, over and above that provided by accounting descriptors, in estimating a stock's residual risk. The authors offer the caveat that their study is in an intermediate stage and suffers from several shortcomings, particularly with regard to the data used. They used annual returns rather than monthly ones, and this may explain why the historical beta was ineffective in predicting the stock's future beta.

In a somewhat different approach, Pettit and Westerfield [1972] argue [pp. 1650-1651] that the variability of an asset's return with the market's return is a function of: (a) the variability of the asset's cash flow with the market's cash flow and (b) the variability of the asset's capitalization rate with the market's capitalization rate. In other words, the risk of holding an asset is related to the expected changes in the investor's portfolio cash flow and the rate at which that flow will be capitalized. These in turn are attributed to the changes in the asset's cash flow and capitalization rate. They found weak empirical evidence that this relationship holds. However, these tests are subject to several serious measurement problems which the authors themselves pointed out. They also compared the explanatory power of traditional accounting variables with the cash flow and capitalization rate variables in explaining individual firm betas and found that the second set of variables was better.

Of course, other surrogates for risk such as Standard and Poor's earnings and dividend rankings or bond quality ratings might be used instead. (See Wagner and Lau, [1971].)

To the extent individuals are (or can become) sufficiently diversified that such risk predictions are of little value, the function of accounting takes on more of its usefulness from a societal viewpoint and needs to be evaluated on its cost of providing information to the entire market relative to alternative information systems. If the accounting system does not provide relevant information (or cause it to be provided), the EMH suggests that alternative information systems will be used. The issue then centers on the cost-benefit analysis of alternative information systems including, but not limited to, accounting systems.[17] Unfortunately, the costs of these alternate systems are not easily determined. They include the costs of collection, storage, processing, and reporting as well as the costs of the arbitrage profits and imposed individual processing costs.

---

[17] On these and related points, see Beaver [1972].

If different information systems produce different equilibria the evaluation process is even more complex.[18]

In a recent study Fama and Laffer [1971] conclude that since the expected value of information generated purely for security trading purposes is zero but requires real resources, production of such information is socially suboptimal. The authors find that the effect of such information is entirely on the distribution of wealth among investors. However, the conclusion follows from the explicit assumptions of their model, and, unfortunately, one of the assumptions required for their model is the assumption of homogenous expectations. This assumption is unlikely to be met. We shall return to this issue in Section 4-5.

The issues we have discussed have implications for accounting research. In particular, they are relevant to the adequacy of tests based on the association of accounting numbers with security prices to establish the informational content of accounting numbers and the use of the association of different accounting alternatives with security prices as a means of establishing a preference ordering among such alternatives.[19] Suppose accounting systems make it economically feasible to supply additional information to the market—information not otherwise available. (Information facilitating interfirm comparisons may provide an example.) Then, in selecting between two alternative systems, the appropriate criterion is the marginal increase in societal benefit achieved from reporting that information not otherwise available, less the difference in cost to society of the two systems. Both the cost and benefit measures must include the net saving (or loss) resulting from the adjustment of those information sources other than the accounting system as well as the costs of the alternate systems described in previous paragraphs.

As May and Sundem [1973] show in some detail, the cost-benefit criterion mentioned above may not be consistent with tests of association between alternative accounting systems and security prices used in some research to date. For example, consider a new accounting information system which will, as does the present one, provide information that would not otherwise be available to the market. Assume, further, that there is some but not complete overlap in these two sets of information. Then to the extent the new system reports additional information not otherwise available, the system may offer an increased benefit to society.

---

[18] Effects due to the change in wealth patterns and those due to long-term consumption patterns appear to require the estimation of society's welfare. To date there is no generally accepted method of accomplishing this task ideal to our purposes. There is some research which suggests that such changes in equilibrium prices should be expected. See May and Sundem [1973].

[19] For example, those raised by Beaver and Dukes [1972].

However, the association between existing security prices and the data that would be reported by the suggested alternative will be lower than with the present reporting system. This is because the additional information in the new system is not presently available to the market and hence it cannot influence prices. (This depends on the assumptions of market rationality with respect to cost.) Finally, it is worth stating that the difficulties of operationalizing the cost and benefit issues suggested here have only recently received some attention in the literature. (See Beaver [1972], Fama and Laffer [1971], and Hirschleifer [1971].)

4-4. NO INDUSTRY EFFECTS: (ASSUMPTION FOUR)

Blume [1970] points out that the market model assumption that the disturbance terms are independent is tantamount to assuming the absence of industry effects. But we would expect such industry effects to exist. King's study [1966] suggests that such effects probably account for only about 10 percent of the variation in monthly returns. Unfortunately, his results are relevant only to long periods. We still have no data with respect to short periods. The modification may not be a serious limitation in measuring the effects of accounting information, but it still adds to the totality of model violations. And what we know very little about is the economic and statistical impact of the simultaneous, although perhaps individually small, violation of several assumptions at once, as is the case here. The industry question suggests a broader issue, namely the adequacy of the expected-returns model. Magee [1974] found that allowing explicitly for the industry factor in earnings yielded better measures of the effect of the earnings of the individual firm on security prices.

4-5. HOMOGENEOUS EXPECTATIONS: (ASSUMPTION FIVE)

An almost universal assumption made by researchers is that investors agree on the implications for equilibrium security prices of any given information set. This is generally known as the assumption of homogeneous expectations. If this is not the case, then a more general statement of the conditions for market equilibrium requires (1) that each investor be in personal equilibrium with respect to his own expectations and (2) that markets are cleared. Under homogeneous expectations both conditions are met. Yet it can be shown, using utility theory, that an individual's utility can be altered by a change in his asset holdings even though the prices of those assets remain fixed.[20]

In a world characterized by heterogeneous expectation, it is not clear how individual investor expectations are aggregated to yield the market's assessment of risk. Under a rather restrictive set of assumptions concerning preferences and probability assessments, Lintner [1965B] has described the aggregation process, but beyond these special situations very little is known.

Lintner [1969] describes the market's aggregation of individual assessments of expected returns and risk. His aggregation model recognizes heterogeneous expectations and indicates how individual probability assessments are aggregated to yield the security's market value. The security's systematic risk, its beta, becomes an ex ante concept specific to each individual. The assessment of a security's beta will differ across individuals with the market reflecting the aggregation over the individual investors comprising the market. We should keep in mind, however, both the restrictions on the probability models allowed and the individual preference functions assumed. Further, the Lintner model is a static model that does not explicitly introduce the concept of information. Finally, this is a theoretical development which, to our knowledge, has not yet been subject to empirical verification.

Rubinstein [1973] separates the claim of the EMH that prices fully reflect information into a set of three increasingly stronger conditions: (1) nonspeculative beliefs, (2) consensus beliefs, and (3) homogeneous beliefs. He states [p.i] that: "After taking an initial portfolio position, an individual is said to perceive *new* information that becomes available to him as fully reflected in revised security prices if and only if he has 'nonspeculative beliefs': beliefs for which no portfolio revision is an optimal strategy. Before taking an initial portfolio position, an individual is said to perceive *all* information that becomes available to him as fully reflected in security prices if and only if he has 'consensus beliefs': beliefs which, if held by all individuals in an otherwise similar economy, would generate the same equilibrium prices as in the actual heterogeneous economy." Rubinstein provides a theoretical argument that even though the first two conditions imply some restrictions on the distribution of security rates of return over time, they are not strong

---

[20] Assuming fixed asset prices is sufficient for the individual investor, but it is not sufficient to locate the market-equilibrium solution. The latter requires a solution for the quantities demanded by each investor plus a set of relative prices that clear the market. Such a solution, while important to the market, is not required for the present point. See Downes and Dyckman [1973].

enough to justify market efficiency, even in its weak form. The assumption of homogeneous beliefs (that is, the assumption that all market participants agree on the implications of information, which is readily available to them at no cost, for the current price and distributions of future prices) is required in order for all individuals to perceive all information fully reflected in security prices.

The role of information as Beaver [1972, p. 408] points out, and to which we referred in Chapter 1, "is two-fold: (1) to aid in establishing a set of security prices, such that there exists an optimal allocation of resources among firms and an optimal allocation of securities among investors, and (2) to aid the individual investor, who faces a given set of prices, in the selection of an optimal portfolio of securities." It is important to distinguish between the securities market and the individual investors that comprise the market, because the role of (accounting) information can be substantively different for each. "To a certain extent, the distinction is artificial, in the sense that the aggregate actions of the individuals determine market behavior. However, the process of aggregation is often deceptive, and if we fail to make the distinction, we may be subject to one of the fallacies of composition. In many cases, what is 'true' for the group as a whole is not 'true' for any individual of that group, and conversely" (p. 408).

If we accept selective perceptions and different information-processing systems on the part of individuals (even among experts), then different expectations should be expected on the basis of different (accounting) information. Note that this in no way implies that there *must* be a change in the equilibrium price.[21] The existence of diverse expectations provides the opportunity for exchanges and the resultant effects on the distribution of wealth and the extent of the external costs created by such transactions including transactions costs, taxes, and any associated opportunity costs.

The importance of individual expectations suggests the importance of research on the volume of trading as well as on price movements. Crouch [1970] provides a theoretical argument for the relationship between volume of transactions and price changes. Shifts in demand for a particular security result in a rise in the number of transactions and either a rise or a fall in the security's price. Crouch points out that

[21]Beaver [1968] has found evidence in the movement of prices in periods of earnings announcements that is consistent with the hypothesis that accounting reports also lead to changes in the equilibrium level of prices. (Note that this makes the evaluation of alternative accounting schemes difficult from a societal viewpoint since some way must be found to evaluate the effects of the different equilibria on the total society.)

studies which test for relationships between price changes and volume generally fail to find significance since the positive and negative price changes tend to cancel each other. However, he shows that the absolute value of price changes regressed on volume yields a significant correlation, and this significance increases as the time period between observations is reduced. These results agree with those of Ying [1966] who found that a large increase in volume is usually accompanied by either a large rise in price or a large fall in price. Beaver [1968] is one of the few accounting investigators to examine volume. He found that volume is approximately 30 percent higher in the week of annual-earnings announcements than during non-report periods. The results are consistent with diverse expectations and the resulting transactions when published data cause reevaluations. The findings also suggest that accounting reports have information content, at least to small investors.

Unfortunately, volume data are subject to availability limitations that seriously limit such tests at the present time. In the first place, a large percentage of the volume in many stocks is transacted outside of organized markets and this activity varies greatly across stocks and hence is not reflected in the published data. It is of relevance to observe that despite the recent increase in daily share volume on the NYSE, the long-run trend in share turnover has been downward. A second concern is with the large block trades that may reflect different decision patterns. Both of these issues provide difficulties in drawing conclusions from volume analyses.

Information contained in accounting reports may at times reinforce the prior expectations of investors, and hence lead to a decrease in the variability of investor expectations. If so, accounting reports provide information which existing tests have no hope of finding.

Further, it is important to recall that the EMH is tested typically using only information with regard to earnings. Yet additional information (say, information on risk) about a firm may be contained in the other data in the financial report. This information may have an impact on market-clearing prices after that of the earnings number which is released earlier to the market. This would help explain why the adjustment process is not instantaneous. The higher than expected price and volume effects after the announcement date noted by Beaver [1968] give support to this notion.

A recent study by Gonedes [1974], however, examined several accounting variables simultaneously, with the results [pp. 38-39] of the "multivariate tests assigning a high probability to the statement that the [accounting] numbers do jointly provide information pertinent to assessing equilibrium expected returns." But, an unexpected result [p. 38] was that the research also assigned "a high probability to the statement that the expected effect of the information jointly reflected in the seven accounting variables (conditional on their multivariate linear discriminant model) differs little from the expected effect of the information reflected in the earnings-per-share variable alone."

There are other *a priori* arguments as to why the adjustment process may not be virtually instantaneous. The effects of some changes such as a new debt issue, may have quite clear effects on the risk-return relationship and hence the adjustment process is nearly instantaneous. Other changes, such as a change in management, may have implications that take more time to produce a market response. The uncertainty surrounding the impact of the information plays a role in the adjustment process. It should be noted, however, that uncertainty by itself does not necessarily imply inefficiency. Fama [1965, p. 39] observes that, "if uncertainty concerning the importance of new information consistently causes the market to underestimate the effect of new information on intrinsic values, astute traders should eventually learn that it is profitable to take this into account."

The assumption of homogeneous expectations implies that all investors are characterized by the same investment horizon. Such an assumption is not likely to reflect the actual state of affairs. H. Levy [1972] presents a theoretical analysis which suggests that one parameter performance measures used in empirical studies will be systematically biased if the study's assumed investment horizon differs from the horizon of investors.

Studies of the impact of accounting numbers have sometimes used monthly data and sometimes yearly data. Yet, in fact, neither of these periods may be an accurate assessment of the investor's horizon. As Levy remarks [1972, p. 651-652], "In most empirical studies which relate to investment in the stock market, the basic unit of time is taken arbitrarily as one year or one month according to the researcher's convenience. But by doing this, the researcher ignores the important role of the basic unit of time for which he calculates rates of return. . . . An empirical study which is based on a yearly rate of return will yield different results from one which uses monthly rate-of-return data. This difference in findings is not a result of inconsistency or contradiction, but is a result of selecting an inappropriate division of the period studied." The resulting systematic bias occurs even if the market is perfect and all the assumptions of the two parameter model hold.

The horizon issue also impacts on the estimation of systematic risk. The issue is whether the estimate of systematic risk needs to be consistent with the horizon of the investor's portfolio. If the answer is yes, then it should be estimated using the same data period (monthly, weekly, etc.) as is used for generating the performance measures. Jensen [1969] has addressed this issue and concluded [p. 191] that the measure of systematic risk is independent of the length of time over which returns are calculated. These results imply that the systematic risk of the portfolio can be estimated without regard for the particular horizon interval for which it is used.

Cheng and Deets [1973] argue to the contrary. They present an analytical development which indicates that the estimate of systematic risk is dependent on the time interval of the data used in the estimation process. They also present empirical evidence which purports to support their analytical development.

However, in a comment on the Cheng and Deets paper, Jacob [1973] points out that the tests made on the empirical results do not seem to reveal anything of major significance for empirical work for either performance measurement or tests of the CAPM, since the differences in the various risk measures appear to be minor. Nevertheless, the results of both the Cheng and Deets work and the paper by Levy suggest that more attention to the horizon issue may be in order if valid conclusions are to be drawn from the empirical research in efficient markets. This conclusion extends to a comparison of the results of studies involving the horizon period.[22]

An implication of heterogeneous expectations is that the effect of accounting information is wider in scope than the traditionally defined user group. The most obvious example is the use of such information by "insiders" in security exchange decisions involving outsiders. But there are wider ramifications in a society where a relatively small group of acknowledged experts interprets the market importance of the information.

Among these implications is the distribution of wealth among the members of society. Different information reporting systems under heterogeneous expectations will affect the distribution of wealth. Furthermore, those affected will not hold the same preferences for information due to the difference in impact of the associated costs and distributive effects. Disagreement will persist as to the net effects to society of changes in an individual's welfare as well as to the implications of given pieces of information.

---

[22] The effects on empirical research results may be even more severe if heterogeneous investor horizons are common and if the assumptions of stationarity and independence over time (the mean and variance of returns are identical over all periods) assumed by these authors in their analytic work are invalid.

In isolated cases, the optimal reporting decision may be selected using the principle of Pareto optimality. (Someone is better off and no one else is worse off.) But in general, such a simple solution will not suffice. The implication is that we need means of measuring the impact on society in the large, and this is not an easy task. Perhaps it also suggests something about the types of issues accountants should address; perhaps attention should now be given more to the extent of disclosure than to the form.

The major argument in this section is, then, that even if we accept the EMH as a reasonable approximation,[23] there are a host of individual effects caused by the heterogeneity of individual expectations that deserve consideration from the accounting viewpoint. Accounting information may have a significantly greater societal impact than some current writers on efficient markets would have us believe. Unfortunately, testing will be difficult in these areas due to both the problems of data availability, disentangling effects of simultaneous information release, and valid cost-benefit measurements.

Given the unrealistic nature of the homogeneous expectations assumption and the limitations it brings to the issues we have addressed, the reader may wonder why writers were content with it. As Stiglitz [1972, p. 459] points out, "the reason that the assumption of identical expectations has been so extensively employed is partly that it is apparently difficult to introduce heterogeneous expectations into such models and still obtain simple results, partly a feeling that one can explain too much too easily in terms of differing expectations, and partly that many of the phenomena which differing expectations might be used to explain can be explained in other terms. For instance, differences in portfolios held by different individuals can be explained by differences both in attitudes toward risk and in expectations. . . . Earlier literature tended to focus on differences in expectations, more recent literature on differences in attitudes towards risk. The reason that different models focus on one or the other is not that either is the 'true explanation'; rather, to understand how each of them works they are best studied in isolation—for example, to understand the effects of differences in attitudes towards risk on portfolio allocation we assume that individuals have the same expectations, and conversely."[24]

---

[23] It might be better to rename the EMH the unbiased-markets hypothesis and save the notion of efficiency for describing the variability of expectations around the equilibrium price.

[24] Stiglitz elected to allow expectations to vary in his research but is then compelled to assume that all individuals have the same risk attitude.

4-6. DATA LIMITATIONS

Testing of the EMH has been largely accomplished by examining the response of a particular stock to particular information. This may not represent an adequate test of the informational effects. The adjustment to information concerning a particular stock may be reflected not only in the price or volume series of that issue but also in those series for other stocks, say, in the same industry. To the extent such multiple stock response is the case, adequate tests of the expected-returns model are more difficult to conduct.

Another way to put the issue is to say that there is a covariance of the earning's residuals among firms with similar betas. This point is related to King's [1966] to the extent similar beta stocks fall into the same industries. But it is more general than King's, both due to its concentration on betas and because, while industries may be composed largely of stocks with similar betas, similar beta stocks are not all grouped in the same industry.

In its most simple form, the point is that the information on the returns of one company may affect the returns of another and the market model does not capture this effect except to the extent it is reflected in the market index. To our knowledge, the importance of this question has not been researched except indirectly by King when he looked at industry effects.

As a final point, we note that the studies of market efficiency have been most commonly done on COMPUSTAT data. The retroactive selection bias introduced by this procedure may be important. An interesting hypothesis would be that a portfolio made up of those firms to be included on the next COMPUSTAT tape would outperform a simply buy-and-hold strategy.

A recent study has been made by Rosenberg and Houglet [1973] on the error rates in the most commonly used data bases namely, the NYSE price tapes produced by the Center for Research in Security Prices (CRSP) at the University of Chicago and the COMPUSTAT data base maintained by Investors Management Sciences of Denver, Colorado. They found that large errors in the reported stock prices were relatively infrequent but did exist and that these few errors were "sufficient to change sharply the apparent nature of the data" for those issues.

4-7. SUMMARY

In this chapter, we have examined the models and assumptions that underlie the empirical research on efficient markets. The CAPM and the market model provide the theoretical justification for empirical research conducted to date. But, as we have seen, there are difficulties with the model assumptions. To the extent the theory is insufficient the empirical work is questionable. Still another problem is the ability of the overall model to support the research based on it. For example, the CAPM specifies the relationships between the expected returns on an asset and the market portfolio. But certain types of accounting changes may alter this equilibrium. An example is an accounting change that alters the economic impact of information-production activities, i.e., a change in who bears the processing cost. A more complete theory may yield substantially different conclusions. These issues together with the empirical research examined in previous chapters, leads us to suggest the usefulness of studies designed not to show *whether or not* the EMH holds, but rather *the degree* to which the hypothesis is valid and useful.

Such studies will not be easy because, in part, of difficulties with the assumptions underlying the related theoretical models as well as the ability of the models to reflect the changes. The studies will also be difficult because of the problem of isolating the portfolio effects of information for individual security issues (and for individuals with different portfolio strategies), and because of the limitations in the availability of volume data. Furthermore, such tests are complicated by the fact that the appropriate cost-benefit measures are both difficult to operationalize, and because the cost-benefit criteria may not be consistent with measures of association between the results of particular information systems and security prices.

Nor should the research stop here. Expected future price changes should be statistically independent of the size of the last transaction and of the earnings change as reflected in quarterly reports, provided only that this information is publicly available under the EMH. The first point suggests that it would be useful to expand the volume studies by segregating large block trades. The investigation of quarterly reporting effects is beginning to receive some attention but the results are fragmentary at this point.[25] It is also perhaps worth pointing out again that most of the empirical research to date has been carried out using only data from the commodity markets and the American and New York Stock Exchanges. There is no reason to believe that the value of accounting information needs to be the same for other less familiar markets such as, for example, regional stock exchanges and the over-the-counter market. One could hypothesize, for example, that for the smaller and less well-known firms that comprise these markets, few (and in some cases maybe no) analysts follow their activities. Given the lags in information distribution, accounting reports may represent important data sources affecting trading. To date the lack of research on such securities means we just don't know.[26]

We have also suggested that a view of the world under homogeneous expectations is too narrow and may lead to the problems of composition. There are, we believe, quite separable issues relating (accounting) information and individual expectations that are of importance in their own right. These include the estimation of expected returns and their resultant importance to investor actions. These issues are neither resolved by the EMH nor have they been adequately considered in adapting the cost-benefit criterion to selection among alternatives.

Having said all this, we still believe the efficient markets research as it bears on financial accounting to represent a significant thrust. Empirical research is by its very nature time-consuming and messy. Conclusions are always subject to reservations. The tendency is to use available data and models and only the wisdom of time and failed replications will generate satisfactory, if not precise, answers to the issues posed by our more comfortable theoretical brothers. Hence we urge expanded empirical research on the adequacy of the theoretical and operational properties of the models used and their application to accounting under the EMH.

In the next and concluding chapter we will attempt to evaluate the present state of this research as it relates to accounting theory and policy formulation. Our discussion will include suggestions for further research.

---

[25] See, for example, May [1971] and Kiger [1972].

[26] In a recently published study Pogue and Solnik [1974] present some tentative results from applying the market model to a broad cross section of European common stocks in several countries. The authors report that, "On the whole, our evidence does not show substantial differences between the United States and the four major European markets [Great Britain, France, Germany, and Italy]. Some cases can be made for the three smaller markets [Belgium, The Netherlands, and Switzerland] being less efficient." It should be noted that a single five-year period [March 1966 to March 1971] is used with preselected security samples involving, with few exceptions, companies with the largest market value in terms of shares outstanding.

CHAPTER FIVE

Implications for Accounting

The objective of this concluding chapter is to place in perspective our knowledge of the efficient market as it relates to accounting. This can best be done by dividing the chapter into five subsidiary questions. They are:

5-1. What are the boundaries of the efficient market as it relates to accounting?

5-2. Is the New York Stock Exchange an efficient market?

5-3. Of what importance and significance is efficiency to the market?

5-4. What implications does market efficiency have for accounting theory and practice?

5-5. What are the implications for accounting research?

Those who have read Chapters 2, 3, and 4 may wish to omit Sections 5-1 and 5-2 of this chapter.

5-1. WHAT ARE THE BOUNDARIES OF THE EFFICIENT MARKET AS IT RELATES TO ACCOUNTING?

The Efficient Market Hypothesis (EMH) is a statement about conditions in the market for securities. In its semi-strong form, which is the strongest form for which there is a substantial body of supportive research, the hypothesis maintains that market equilibrium prices of securities fully reflect all publicly available information. Further, these prices (or returns) react virtually instantaneously and in an unbiased fashion as new information becomes available. We should recognize that this is an extreme statement. One would not expect the hypothesis to be literally true, for example, in the requirement for virtually instantaneous response. But those who accept the EMH do so as a reasonably accurate view of the price adjustment process in the securities market.

The function of the market for securities is three-fold. First, it provides a mechanism for the allocation of capital among ventures. Second, it is a means by which the ownership and management of large and risky ventures can be separated. And third, it functions as an exchange through which individuals can trade dollars for future consumption claims, namely securities, and vice versa. The exchange of dollars for securities involves a gamble concerning the amount of funds available in the future. Through the securities market, individuals 'acting collectively or alone can be viewed as exchanging consumption claims in order to maximize their own utility.

As a statement about the relationship between prices and information in the securities market, the EMH relates only to the prices of publicly held and traded securities. Hence, it incorporates only a segment, albeit a large and important one, of economic activity. Excluded, for example, are all nonprofit activities and closely held profit-seeking corporations.

In its more general form the hypothesis can be extended to cover any organized market, such as the markets for government obligations, corporate bonds, and commodities. However, with only a few notable exceptions, empirical studies have been confined to the securities market, and in particular to the New York Stock Exchange. But even this broader interpretation of organized markets omits several significant types of alternative investments, including savings accounts, real estate, and works of art, although these, too, could be included.

The role of information in the efficient market theory is two-fold.

First, it is central to setting the relative security price structure, thereby playing a vital role in the allocation of resources among firms and securities among individuals. Second, it assists individuals in selecting the best portfolio for their needs.

An examination of the role of information is typically confined to that information, transmitted to the securities market via accounting numbers, which either is or can be made available under current practice and technology. This examination has emphasized the results of transactions at the aggregate rather than at the individual investor level. The emphasis is on the price structure or the relative prices of securities vis-à-vis one another in a state of equilibrium. This reflects the fact that the EMH makes no statements concerning either the volume of trading or the effects on individual investors.

Focus on the securities market also means that the EMH pertains to what accountants call external reporting. The EMH has nothing directly to say about internal (or management) accounting. Indirectly, of course, internal and external reporting are related. Data gathered for internal purposes are often used to prepare reports for external use. Further, the effect or perceived effect of the externally reported accounting numbers on the market price of the stock can influence the internal operating decision which led to the accounting data. Some anecdotal evidence to this effect is cited by Beaver [1973] and by Dyckman [1971]. Nevertheless, the EMH is not directed toward the effects of internal accounting reports. Hence, were we to accept the EMH, we should keep in mind that it is relevant to only a limited (if important) portion of the field of accounting.

We mentioned that the EMH is concerned primarily with the operation of the securities market at the macro or aggregate level. A clear distinction is drawn between the securities market per se and the individual investors who comprise the market. The distinction is important since the role of information in each context, for the market and for the individual, can be quite different. This does not mean that the EMH has no significant implications for individual behavior, but rather that these implications are a consequence of accepting the theory. The theory itself does not attempt to explain market behavior through an aggregation of individual behavior. At a later point, we will suggest that relying on aggregate behavior alone may cause the role of accounting information to be underestimated.

The EMH, when confined to securities, restricts the empirical analysis to those organizations whose stocks are traded in organized markets. Investment opportunities other than securities in such organizations are not considered. In accounting research, information reaching the market is limited to that contained in accounting numbers (although empirical research has considered other types of information such as stock splits, stock dividends, secondary offerings, and rights). Concentration on the impact of accounting information on the equilibrium price structure within organized securities markets omits from consideration much of the information content of accounting reports generated for internal decisions, as well as for external purposes other than setting security prices. Moreover, empirical research has often concentrated on the earnings numbers alone to the exclusion of other data contained in formal accounting reports. On the other hand, a study by Gonedes [1974] suggests that although several accounting numbers considered jointly provide information pertinent to assessing equilibrium returns, the results differ little from those obtained using only earnings per share.

Nevertheless, we should keep in mind that accounting data find their way into many important economic activities other than capital market decisions. The obtaining of credit, tax reporting, labor contracts and negotiations, economic research supporting governmental policy decisions, legal proceedings including (but not limited to) antitrust cases, and regulatory reporting requirements are indicative but not exhaustive of these important uses of accounting data. We do not yet know, nor has anyone investigated, the implications, if any, of the efficient market research for these decisions. We believe that reporting decisions in these areas will continue to be strongly influenced by considerations outside the boundaries of the EMH.

These restrictions and the aggregate market focus of the EMH should be remembered when evaluating both the importance of accounting information and the policy implications for setting accounting standards based on accepting the EMH.

5-2. IS THE NEW YORK STOCK EXCHANGE AN EFFICIENT MARKET?

As has been indicated, the EMH is a statement about the functioning of organized markets for securities. The best known of these markets is the New York Stock Exchange. Until recently, only data from the NYSE existed in adequate amounts and in a form readily accessible to researchers interested in empirical tests of the EMH. Hence, nearly all published research applies to the NYSE alone. Since very few studies have been made of other markets, any conclusions about the efficiency of the NYSE can be extrapolated only with some chance of error to other organized markets. Firms listed on the NYSE are different from firms listed on other organized markets in several ways, including size and diversity of ownership. It is possible that these firm differences are related to market differences. Such market differences could occur if insufficient attention is given to these markets by investors and analysts.

Chapter 2 examined a number of empirical studies generally supportive of semi-strong form efficiency in the NYSE. The conclusions of these studies, as is true in general of all empirical research, are subject to limitations, which stem from two major sources. First, there is the contradictory empirical evidence (reviewed in Chapter 3) based on the implications of the EMH. Second, there are unresolved issues (discussed in Chapter 4) concerning the underlying theory and the assumptions of the economic models used in the empirical tests.

Turning to the first type of limitation, an efficient market implies that security trading systems based on observed prices (or returns) will not consistently permit abnormal returns—returns above those commensurate with the security's risk. This is the so-called "fair-game" property of the hypothesis. Secondly, deviations of actual returns from expectations should not be predictable. (In formal terms, the serial covariances of the residual return series should have zero expectations for all lags.) Further, the market should exhibit essentially an instantaneous and unbiased response of security prices to new information.

Although, as we saw in Chapter 2, there is a substantial body of research that finds in favor of the efficient market using each of these sets of implications, Chapter 3 reviews several contrary studies. But these latter studies, too, are subject to limitations. The more important of these limitations relate to the common failure of many of the contradictory studies to allow for one or more of the following factors: risk, information costs, and transaction costs. Often it is not clear if the apparently documented inefficiency would still exist if allowance for these factors were properly made.

The second set of limitations relates to the requirements of the economic world assumed to underlie the efficient market. The model of the economic environment employed in these tests assumes, in part, a relatively simple two parameter world in which only the mean and variance of the distribution of portfolio returns are relevant to investors. Investors are assumed to be averse to risk (as opposed to those such as gamblers, who have a preference for it) and to be concerned with maximizing the expected utility of their wealth. These same investors are also assumed to have identical expectations concerning the average returns on every security, the variability of the return, and the relationship of the movement of each security's return to the movement of the returns on all other securities. Investors are price takers with free access to information. They can trade a given asset stock without concern for transaction costs. Finally, it is assumed that investors can lend and borrow unlimited amounts at the same risk-free interest rate over which they have no influence. These assumptions have been made to simplify the underlying complexity of the subject to be researched, a necessary step in understanding any "real world" phenomenon.

Although these assumptions appear overwhelming in their simplification, many of them have allowed a better understanding of the securities market without doing unwarranted violence to the operational validity of the world they purport to describe. However, as we saw in Chapter 4, several of these assumptions have received considerable attention recently. There is now discussion of whether or not individual investors can borrow unlimited amounts at a risk-free rate. If they cannot, a more accurate (and perhaps complex) description of the world is needed before valid tests of the EMH are possible. The two parameter (mean-variance) model may not capture sufficient richness to justify its use. It may be necessary, for example, to consider skewness. However, at this time there is no general agreement concerning the value of these more complex descriptions of the process generating security returns.

Among the many simplifying assumptions, that of homogeneous expectations stands out. We know it is a poor description of reality, but we have not to date adequately examined its impact on tests of the efficient market. We do know that it can affect empirical tests. At one level the assumption is that investors have identical, homogeneous investment horizons. If this is not the case or if some horizon other than that relevant to investors is used, measures of performance (such as rates of return) will be systematically biased. This produces what appears to be (but in fact may not be) conflicting results from empirical studies that use different data time periods.

Furthermore, this assumption also deals with important differences among individual investors, while the focus of accounting information studies has been at the aggregate market level. Although the EMH, if accepted, has implications for individual investors, the importance of information and, in particular, accounting information will be underestimated if only a total market approach is utilized, even for securities markets. Just as the process of aggregation can lead to the fallacy of composition, so the process of disaggregation can lead to the fallacy of composition. The fact that the market is efficient says nothing about the process of individual trading or the dynamics of the process which produces market efficiency. The importance of this process to the valuation of accounting information is a topic to which we will return later.

The assumption of risk-averse investors implies that there is a positive (or direct) relationship between expected security returns and risk:

high risk implies a high expected return. The economic theory that has been used to relate risk and return, the market model, assumes that the expected return on a security is equal to a constant (the risk-free rate for borrowing or lending) plus an additive term for the security's risk. The risk term is made up of an index of the return on the total market and a multiplier which is different for each stock. The greater a stock's risk, the larger the multiplier. (The stock's risk is measured not by the variability of its own return, but rather by the ratio of the variability of its return with the market return—its covariance with the market return—to the variability of the market return.)

This assumed economic description of the relationship of risk and return is used to generate data for testing the EMH. In so doing, it is necessary to estimate the risk multiplier or risk coefficient, called the stock's beta coefficient, for each stock considered. The estimation process typically used has assumed a stock's beta coefficient to be constant over time. Although such an assumption appears warranted for the risk coefficient of a portfolio of, say, ten or more stocks, there is substantial evidence as well as logic which indicates that this assumption is a poor description of a single stock's risk coefficient over time.

For investors with either small or risk-similar holdings, changes in a stock's beta value can lead to transaction and information costs as these investors attempt to adjust their holdings to reflect their risk-return strategy. This is particularly true for investors who may wish to pursue high-risk strategies. Moreover, a lack of diversification is not uncommon among investors holding stocks traded on the NYSE. But of greater importance to the validity of the EMH is the effect of changing security beta values on empirical testing. Empirical tests have often been conducted using the returns on individual securities. To examine the effect of accounting information which is stock specific, it is necessary to remove from a stock's return series the effects of general economic events. This is accomplished for each period and for each stock by subtracting the market effect as represented by the product of the market index with the stock's beta value. A constant beta for each stock over time has traditionally been used. To the extent the stock's beta changes over time (as it would if the firm's risk were to change) and this is ignored in the above process, the return series generated is in error and the empirical tests based on the resultant data are suspect. The effects of such movements over time, if not systematic, would, however, tend to cancel out for moderate to large portfolios, thus reducing this problem's significance.

So where does an examination of the empirical evidence leave us? If one's prior beliefs in an efficient market were strong, he will not find sufficient evidence to reject the theory. On the other hand, there is sufficient evidence to soothe the skeptic as well. But this is simply because we have asked the wrong questions. The issue is not whether the market—in particular, given past empirical work, the NYSE—is efficient or not, but rather the issue at this level is *how* efficient is this market and of what importance is the efficiency. Once phrased in this way, researchers may begin to examine the degree of efficiency in the market and the dynamics by which this efficiency is manifested. Questions of the time delay of information processing, perhaps operationalized using concepts such as the half-life of information (the time required for half the information effect to be reflected in the market), take on importance. Further, we could begin to make the subtle but important distinctions between the life and value of different types of information bits. Moreover, different markets will in all likelihood be characterized by different degrees of efficiency. Regional stock exchanges and the over-the-counter market may have different and, possibly, lower degrees of efficiency when compared to the NYSE, perhaps due to higher transactions costs, thinner markets, etc.

Furthermore, we should learn to investigate the value of accounting information not only in terms of its global effects on different potential market equilibria but also in terms of its impact on individuals. We should consider other uses to which accounting information may be put such as the assessment of a security's risk. And we need to know the cost and benefits to society from reporting information via the accounting framework as compared to other possible information sources. Finally, we need to examine the relationships between disclosure and the monopoly profits that accrue to those with inside information.

5-3. OF WHAT IMPORTANCE AND SIGNIFICANCE IS EFFICIENCY TO THE MARKET?

In the first place, an efficient market is a desirable state of affairs for society. To the extent that the market is efficient, securities are appropriately priced relative to one another based on publicly available information. The allocation of scarce resources among activities in such a market situation should be more nearly optimal than when no such relationship exists among security prices. Furthermore, no group of individual investors is placed at a disadvantage in such a market. To the extent that prices reflect all available information virtually instantaneously, individuals need not concern themselves with the search for over- and under-valued stocks, unless, of course, they possess information no one else has.

We should keep in mind, however, that the EMH gives only a general statement of equilibrium return behavior. In practice the market is constantly moving from one approximate equilibrium to another. In so doing, there will always be at least brief inefficiencies in the market. Indeed, it is in part a belief in the existence of these inefficiencies and the net benefit available from their discovery that hastens the adjustment process. If everyone were to believe in the instantaneous theory of adjustment, the degree of efficiency in the market would quickly dissipate, at least momentarily. Thus, both the belief in at least some degree of inefficiency when new information becomes available, and the costs associated with search and action, are necessary to retain efficiency in the market. The implications for specialists and brokers who are continually searching for inefficiencies and the value of the activities of these individuals to the market is clear, as is the importance of the perspicacity with which individuals find new and better ways to perform their tasks.

We need also to recognize again the partial nature of the hypothesis as it is applied to capital markets. Optimal resource allocation need not be a characteristic of an economy where security markets are (but other investment markets are not) efficient. Moreover, the measurement and definition of optimality create additional problems. As several writers have pointed out, Beaver [1972] for example, an economy-wide optimal resource allocation requires the measurement of the increase in societal welfare compared to the costs of alternate total information systems, of which accounting is only a part. This portends substantial research problems that have not been adequately investigated at this time.

Security prices and price changes affect the distribution of wealth and the related overall well-being of individuals. Since the total information system creates the forces leading to an equilibrium set of prices, it is entirely possible, as researchers in this area have indicated, Beaver [1972], that alternate information systems could lead to different sets of market-clearing prices. Means by which such alternate equilibria can be predicted and their total impact on society evaluated do not yet exist. If or when several information systems lead to essentially the same market-clearing prices, then a choice among them can be based on an assessment of the cost of the system including the costs of data collection, processing, storage, retrieval, and dissemination, as well as the monopoly profits arising in the arbitrage process and transaction costs. However, to the extent that such costs fall differently on individuals, the cost evaluation process reflects the same social welfare issues as exist in estimating the benefits.

Accounting, it must be borne in mind, is only one element in the total information system. It has no monopoly on supplying information to the market. If the data it supplies become redundant or too costly for investors to use, it can be replaced by alternate sources. (This will occur in an efficient market.) A question researchers should ask about accounting information is, does it supply relevant information and, if so, do alternate accounting procedures yield the same information? If so, the least expensive means of providing the relevant information should be used. (In determining the least-cost alternative, differences in individual investor processing costs should be counted.) We need to learn just where accounting data have an overall comparative advantage in supplying information to the market.

5-4. WHAT IMPLICATIONS DOES MARKET EFFICIENCY HAVE FOR ACCOUNTING THEORY AND PRACTICE?

Semi-strong market efficiency has several implications for accounting visibility issues. Since information is publicly available even if it is only reported in a footnote to the published financial statements, or in a 10-K annual report to the Securities and Exchange Commission, market efficiency would predict that such information would be properly impounded in security prices. Further, any subsequent disclosure of such information in a more visible manner, for example, a diversified company disclosing product line information in its annual reports when the information is already in the 10-K, would not cause the security's price to change.

In addition, when there is an easy way to convert from one accounting method to another, and the costs of conversion are insignificant, but it is not possible to convert from the second back to the first (as can be the case with deferral and flow-through earnings measures), then the first method should be reported, since any investors who want the second method will be able to convert the reported numbers. Then market efficiency will guarantee that all information contained in both measures will be promptly and properly reflected in the security price. But the impact of market efficiency does not cease here.

For example, it can be argued that even if prices do not change, that is, the same market equilibrium prices exist, alternative reporting methods may produce a change in the process by which this equilibrium is achieved. Such a change could, for example, entail more or less trading with the resultant effects on individuals or a change in the distribution of the profits arising from the necessary arbitrage operations. If this is so, the EMH may be relevant to a selection among the reporting alternatives that lead to the alternate equilibrium processes.

From an accounting standpoint, the research on the EMH has also provided two important means by which a better understanding of the role of external accounting information can be obtained. First, it has provided a set of research methods by which relationships between accounting information and security prices can be studied. Second, and of equal importance, it has provided both an economic rationale for using the related research techniques and a justification for such studies. Too often theoretical developments and empirical testing go their independent ways. Yet each is equally important and together they substantially improve the chances of obtaining valid and useful insights into the functioning of actual phenomena. From this viewpoint the efficient market research thread is more complete than most other research methodologies.

Yet one must be careful in suggesting that such analysis alone can lead to the resolution of accounting-policy disagreements. Beaver and Dukes [1972], for example, suggest using the accounting method most highly associated with security prices, subject to cost-benefit considerations. Their approach is based on the acceptance of efficiency in the market. If the market is efficient, then security prices reflect the available information. To facilitate the process, where two ways of reporting the same information exist, it is logical to report the information that seems to be impounded in prices, namely, that most consistent with the information set underlying security prices. In this way the (efficient) market indirectly indicates the preferred reporting method.

Despite the attractiveness of appealing to the market, several reasons for caution exist. First, the supportive empirical research must assume or argue away the confounding effects of variables that cannot be controlled and which are varying simultaneously; this, of course, requires that such possible influences be detected at some (hopefully early) stage of the investigation. Existing studies which use empirical research to suggest policy choices are subject to this limitation. Second, the limitations to the research methodologies embodied in the economic models discussed in Chapter 4 also apply to these studies in varying degrees. Third, the total analysis is a partial one, even as to the information system. In other words, accounting is only a part of the total information system and the securities market is only a part of the total market for assets. As a result, the market may obtain the information from another source.

Further, the choice among alternative accounting methods involves, as Beaver [1973] and others recognized, a choice among different consequences in terms of the cost and benefits. Different individuals experience differential effects in terms of how well off they are under these choices. Hence to make a choice among accounting alternatives results in social effects we do not yet know how to measure. This issue, one we have mentioned before, requires resolution before optimal choices can be made.

In addition, the research methodology employed is not always adequate to support the conclusions suggested. May and Sundem [1973] have pointed to an important limitation in this approach. Consider a new accounting information system based on replacement cost that provides, as does the existing one based on historical cost, information not otherwise available to the market. Suppose further that there is some, but not complete, overlap in the information supplied by the two systems. The new system may benefit society to the extent it reports new information not otherwise available. Yet it is possible that the association between security prices and measures supplied by the proposed system will be lower, since the potential new information is not presently available to the market.

In a still more recent paper Beaver and Demski [1974, p. 10] recognize these problems in stating that an association test cannot "in and of itself imply or dictate a preference for one reporting practice over another." We must also recognize that, to make these judgments, the market price must reflect the value of the information production activities. Beaver [1974, p. 570] puts it succinctly when he writes, "although evidence [in particular association tests between accounting data and security price behavior] cannot indicate what choice to make, it can provide information on the potential consequences of various choices. . . . The ultimate issue is the extent to which this simplified preference ordering [for accounting reporting alternatives] is consistent with the ordering obtained under a complete analysis."

In the present institutional framework, where accounting policy is decided by political processes, decisions are made on the basis of the policy-makers' beliefs concerning the effects of alternative accounting procedures on the securities markets and investors. As examples, separate disclosure of extraordinary items in the income statement is based on a belief that such items are of importance to the market. Many arguments presented during the FASB hearings on the methods of accounting for leases were based on beliefs concerning the effects of lease capitalization on the securities markets. In addition, arguments in favor of line-of-business reporting are usually based on the belief that such disclosure would affect investor decisions and security prices. In all these cases, the choice of an accounting alternative is to an extent dependent on beliefs concerning the effects of the alternatives on security prices, and the degree to which these beliefs reflect reality is essentially an empirical question. Therefore, research concerning the effects of extraordinary items, lease capitalization or line-of-business reporting on security prices can provide helpful information to an accounting policy-maker. For example, the SEC requirement that significant lease obligations and the effect of their capitalization on income be disclosed in a footnote combined with the EMH implication that such information will already be reflected in security prices could be used by FASB members in evaluating arguments based on beliefs concerning the effects of lease capitalization on security prices.

As pointed out above, the EMH insures that all (public) information will be reflected in security prices. Therefore, a researcher may use the association between an accounting item and security prices to make an inference about the effect of that accounting item on security prices. A further inference about the effect of that accounting item on individual investors cannot generally be made without assuming a very specific environment. Therefore, a market association can provide a policy-maker with *some* of the effects of an accounting alternative, but not *all* the effects.

This type of research, then, is necessary to determine whether the market is using the information transmitted by a particular accounting technique. But it is not sufficient for this purpose, since the market may get the information from other sources or noise may prevent the researcher from identifying the effect. Nor is this type of research sufficient to select the best technique. Costs must also be considered and benefits must be approximated. Yet at this time the measurement problems are unresolved.

Gonedes and Dopuch [1974] present a theoretical framework which includes the effects of information-production decisions on capital market equilibrium. They also conclude that under the present institutional system, in which accounting information is made available without charge, the prices of firms' securities cannot be used in association tests to assess the relative desirability of alternative accounting procedures. However, it is possible according to these authors to use security prices to measure the effects of the accounting data, as was done in the studies by Ball and Brown [1968] and by Kaplan and Roll [1972] described in Chapter 2.

If the market mechanism cannot be used, for whatever reasons, to evaluate alternative accounting methods, we must turn elsewhere. The possibilities include political systems involving either dictatorial imposition or voting schemes. One such political organization is the SEC and another is the FASB. Accounting theory will play a role in the deliberations of these bodies but other pressures will also be important as the history of the SEC and the APB (the FASB's predecessor) suggest.

Some but not enough research has been done in evaluating these and similar alternatives. The issue is complex since it also entails issues of social choice and social welfare.

Care should also be taken in using the efficient market literature and techniques as a basis for selecting research topics. We have an uneasy feeling that the attractiveness of research topics in this area is fostered in substantial part by the availability of the data base in the form of stock market and accounting data tapes. The only study of which we are aware on the accuracy of these data, Rosenberg and Houglet [1973], indicates the existence of a very low error rate for stock prices. However, the effect of these errors on the summary statistics for the individual issues in question was dramatic. Moreover, to the best of our knowledge, no study of the accuracy of the accounting data contained on these tapes has been made. The possibility exists that the error level may be substantial.

A more modest goal of the research efforts in accounting and efficient markets has been to see if accounting provides information to the market. The answer is somewhat ambiguous. Studies indicate a market reaction that is anticipatory to the release of accounting data. Accounting reports do not possess a monopoly on these data and competing sources may scoop their formal release. But while this finding may diminish the perceived information content of accounting reports, it is nevertheless consistent with the information content of the accounting process leading to these reports. Either the market reacts to the accounting process or it behaves in a consistent manner for other reasons. Perhaps, for biased reasons, we choose to accept the apparent support for the information content provided by the accounting process.

Yet we would go further. If we examine again the role of the individual investor, we find additional indications of the importance of accounting information.

Accounting researchers who tend to accept the EMH stress the relevance of accounting data to estimating risk, as reflected in the beta coefficient, of individual securities. Well-diversified investors in an efficient market require such information in order to adjust their portfolio to the desired risk-return relationship. However, a substantial number of individual investors are not well diversified, and there is no a priori reason to assume such behavior irrational, particularly if the world is not adequately reflected by the simplified economic models which support the EMH. Under such conditions good information concerning risk takes on increased importance if investors are to minimize transaction costs while retaining their desired portfolio strategy involving risk and return.

These individuals also need to estimate future returns if the desired risk-return relationship is to be maintained. It is important to note that errors in the accounting data could lead to different valuations by different individuals, once the assumption of homogeneous expectations is dropped. Again, this leads to an increase in transactions costs and hence to effects on individual well-being. Thus, we conclude, contrary to some writers, including Beaver [1972], that prediction errors in the return distributions of several individual securities due to the accounting reporting rules can have undesirable side effects and should not be ignored because (some) investors may be able to diversify out of them. The point is magnified when we recall that stocks do not always reflect the values they should. Partly this is due to the dynamics of the market-adjustment process and partly to the fact that the actual situation in a company may be concealed for a time as was true for Penn Central, Lockheed, and Equity Funding. In these cases (and others) a substantial number of individual investors were adversely affected. Yet this took place in an efficient market. ' The security price adjustments were nearly immediate once the news was made public. In this case the actual situation may have been known only to insiders.

In paraphrasing Beaver on prediction errors, we should observe that once an individual holds more than a single security, the unsystematic risk of that portfolio is less than the weighted average of the unsystematic risk of the individual securities. Beaver [1974, p. 569] argues that accounting issues should be viewed at the portfolio rather than at the individual level. "Nondiversification at the individual investor level is not sufficient to warrant a consideration of unsystematic risk when making information policy decisions. It is important to distinguish between the private value of information (which considers one investor in isolation) and the social value of information (which considers all investors in the market). While an individual investor may be willing to pay to reduce his unsystematic risk, this in no way implies that society as a whole would be willing to expend real resources in the same manner."

The point is that efficiency in the securities market has nothing to say about the quantity or the quality of accounting information. The issue of what accounting information is desired by individuals remains whether the market is efficient or not. The question here is rather one of the efficiency of the information-production process.

There are a priori reasons to believe that the market may react with different speed to different kinds of information. For example, some changes, such as a new debt issue, have an immediately recognizable effect on a security's risk. The effects of other changes, such as a change in management, may not be immediately obvious.[1] Again, differential evaluations are likely in the latter case with the concurrent effects on transactions costs and individual well-being. Furthermore, it is important to go beyond the change itself to find the reason for the change if meaningful reporting implications are to be reached and mitigating changes suggested.

The net result is that even if the equilibrium price structure in the market does reflect all publicly available information—in this sense the price structure is unbiased—there will remain a dispersion of individual expectations around what can be thought of as the market's average response. This distribution of expectations leads to transactions, and hence to transactions costs.[2] If an alternate (accounting) information system could decrease the dispersion of individual expectations, it would represent an improvement in the operation of the market by decreasing transactions (subject, of course, to cost considerations). In other words, research on the process by which individuals process information is still very relevant.

On the policy side, to the extent we can accept the EMH, accounting policy should aim to increase investor awareness of the fact that reported accounting data are not likely to be useful in detecting over- or undervalued securities. Searching for such securities simply leads to increased transaction costs, the likelihood of improper diversification, and the possibility of a portfolio with inappropriate risk characteristics.

We can all agree that publicly held corporations should provide the market and those who act within it the best possible information subject to cost considerations. Further, the corporation should disseminate this information as widely as possible (again cost considerations are relevant) so that the well being of some will not be adversely affected relative to others because the latter receive the information first. (We are ignoring the case of those who can, by virtue of their position, act quicker, such as speculators.) But these statements do not address the accounting issues of major importance and difficulty such as what reporting areas warrant concern, what reporting methods should be used in these areas, whether differences should be allowed within industries, at what point

---

[1] If uncertainty concerning the importance of new information causes a consistent underestimate of a security's intrinsic value, astute traders should eventually take this into account.

[2] Research on the issue of excessive transactions costs might well focus on the volume of activity rather than simply on returns. We spoke of this issue in Chapter 4.

the information-processing activity should be turned over to individuals, to what extent useful measures of social benefits and costs can be quantified, and so on.

In particular, issues dealing with information that has a nontrivial additional cost if reported by different media represent important policy areas and hence areas for research. In such cases, even though it is more costly, information should be reported via the accounting statements if the benefits in terms of decreased insider abnormal returns and a lower cost for providing the information through other media, exceed the additional reporting costs. Even if reporting via accounting statements is less expensive, other media should be used if the benefits in terms of lower total transaction costs and improved portfolio risk at the individual level exceed the savings in lower reporting costs and the benefits to such reporting mentioned in the previous sentence. Because some investors will be better off and others worse under different information systems, some aggregate social measure is, however, once again required before definitive conclusions are possible.

Reporting questions also remain for the choice among accounting procedures. However, if there is essentially no additional cost either to the firm from reporting information in the accounting statements under one reporting alternative versus another, nor to the investor in converting from one to the other, there is a strong a priori case for disclosure of the figures necessary to make the conversion. Examples include interperiod tax allocation, accounting for unmarketable securities, the investment credit, and earnings per share under convertible securities. As Beaver [1973] observes, too much policy-level effort has been devoted to these kinds of problems. One of the more striking examples involves the insurance industry, which opposes including information on marketable securities in the income statement even though market values are already reported on the balance sheet.

The case for disclosure is strengthened when one recognizes that failure to disclose may result in insider information which can lead to monopolistic profits for those who hold it. Disclosure should be the rule unless it can be convincingly demonstrated that no abnormal returns can be earned or that disclosure cost exceeds any expected abnormal returns. Thus although lack of disclosure can lead to speculative profits and, hence, a cost to society, disclosure may not be the solution. This suggests that one important area for further research involves attempts to measure the costs of additional disclosure and the impact of such disclosure on security prices and society welfare. This would lead inevitably to a consideration of the extent to which nonpublished data is currently reflected in asset prices.[3]

These arguments extend directly to many perplexing issues. For example, it is possible to define the accountant's legal liability in terms of insufficient disclosure where insufficient disclosure is itself defined in terms of the occurrence (or reasonable expectation of occurrence) of an abnormal return in excess of the disclosure cost. Similarly, an efficient market will decide the relevance of certified forecast data. A failure to disclose such data or attest to it may simply protect insider information sources and hence create monopoly profits. (See Beaver [1973].)

We have also observed that it is partly the belief in inefficiencies or at least in some friction in the market that causes the individual (professional) search activity necessary to attain whatever degree of efficiency exists. This is the case of a hypothesis which, if believed, fails. Only if a sufficient number of doubters exists can some degree of efficiency be maintained.

Finally, of course, we can enumerate other uses of accounting information, for external as well as internal purposes, which should be considered in any program of evaluation or policy prescription. These additional external uses include: union contract negotiations, the impact of events on the community and the larger environment, loan applications, merger and aquisition transactions, license applications, reports to regulatory agencies, and so on.

5-5. WHAT ARE THE IMPLICATIONS FOR ACCOUNTING RESEARCH?

We have from time to time in this book suggested fruitful areas of research. For example, in Section 5-4 we observed that research on the means by which individuals process information is very relevant. Other suggestions included encouragement to those trying to develop better expectation models and improved means of specifying the appropriate relationships between individual security returns; further research involving the volume of trading; and means of capturing the impact of alternate reporting systems on the welfare of society. Chapters Two and Three

---

[3] Benston (1967), examining the Securities Exchange Act of 1934 by using an efficient market test procedure similar to Ball and Brown's (1968), concludes, p. 153, that the Act "had no measurable positive effect on the securities traded on the NYSE. There appears to have been little basis for the legislation and no evidence that it was needed or desirable. Certainly there is doubt that more required disclosure is warranted." Yet, even if we accept Benston's conclusions as they relate to market efficiency, the above case for disclosure remains intact.

suggested that additional studies based on the implications of efficiency are still in order. In Chapter Four we discussed research concerning the validity of the models underlying the EMH. The validity of these models is at best an unresolved empirical issue. At present, further research into the issue of skewness and its relationship to financial statement variables is needed.

Another major research area concerns what can be done once we accept heterogeneous individual decision makers with diverse preferences and beliefs. Demski [1973 and 1974] has begun to address this question in the context of individual consumption decisions within the framework of the economy-wide model used in general equilibrium theory (see, for example, Arrow and Hahn [1971]). This system has the advantage not only of focussing on individual consumption decisions but of incorporating both financial statement users and nonusers.

The role of (financial statement) information in this model is to alter the individual's beliefs concerning the states of the world in which consumption decisions will be made. The results of applying this analysis are unsettling. They show that any attempt to rely on standards (such as objectivity, fairness, verifiability or—more esoterically—aggregation and information theory) will not ensure a normative theory of accounting. As Demski [1974, p. 228] observes, "the question of what we mean by an optimal set of financial reporting systems cannot be approached by assimilating individual preferences and opinions in a manner consistent with Arrow's condition." [4] Nor can one fall back on reports for specific classes of users since one set of users may be harmed by reporting that benefits an alternate group.

The result is an inevitable tradeoff of gains and losses among financial statement users. This suggests several research areas including: (1) the attempts to specify those areas in which acceptable social evaluations can be made; (2) the delineation of accounting changes that are associated with a change in incidence of information production costs and, hence, with the distribution of wealth (which, in turn, requires the evaluation of societal effects); (3) the investigation of biases within policy-influencing organizations; and (4) the nature of interpersonal tradeoffs occasioned by the imposition of alternate accounting reporting standards. "In short" as Demski [1974, p. 232] observes, "fundamental questions of resource allocation and social choice appear to underlie the question of choice among financial reporting alternatives. Hopefully accounting theory one

---

[4] Arrow's famous impossibility theorem states that there is no method of selecting among social alternatives which is not dictatorial, but is Pareto optimal, independent of irrelevant alternatives, and which provides a complete, transitive, and reflexive ranking of the social alternatives. (See Arrow [1963] and Demski [1974] p. 228.)

day will account for these phenomena." The usefulness of the EMH in the research strategies suggested in this section is that it assists us in assessing the effects of alternate reporting techniques. Such knowledge is central to the decision making process of those in policy positions. Finally, given the numerous alternate uses of accounting data in internal and external decision making, we in no way wish to imply a diminution in this important research trust.

5-6. SUMMARY

The research in accounting spawned by the EMH, and supported by research in finance on portfolio theory and capital asset pricing, has made substantive contributions to both accounting research methodology and the logic of the issues investigated. It does a much needed task of tying empirical research to theory and showing the relevance of the issues addressed to a complete program of accounting research. Yet, as we have seen, this strand of analysis covers only a segment, albeit an important one, of the total economic activity to which even the accounting information system relates.

True, it is a source of testable hypotheses, but it is not unique in this regard. Recommendations for accounting policy should not be based solely on the findings of such research efforts even if these findings can be accepted. Such policy decisions involve moral judgments as well. The information desires of individuals remain even in an efficient market. Given an efficient market, we can tell at most the consequences of various policy decisions. And at this point the research results themselves remain open to question. Theory must become more global and testing more accurate and complete before broad accounting policy solutions can stand adequately on the resulting foundation. Until that time, accountants will continue to find sufficient reasons to support different solutions to accounting problems. One's choice will hinge largely on one's prior beliefs in the adequacy of the underlying theory, the validity of the supportive research, the practical implication of one's choice of an information system and its impact on social welfare and economic activity, and the costs (political and other) of implementation.

Yet theory (analytical or otherwise), although necessary, is not sufficient to resolve accounting policy issues. While the empirical research on efficient markets is still incomplete, it would be a mistake to ignore its tentative findings and establish policy without regard to the issues it raises. Indeed in some areas, for example, disclosure of information on the market value of marketable securities, the presumption at this time would favor the efficient market conclusion. Namely, disclosure is appropriate. Research in efficient markets has also added to the implements we have to address these issues, but it has not and will not solve all reporting problems. Proponents of the EMH and its implications often claim too much while its detractors give it too little. As with most innovations, the truth lies nearer the middle ground.

APPENDIX A

Expectation, Variance, Covariance, and Skewness

Each of these terms finds extensive use in the efficient market literature. For this reason, the reader must understand them at least at an intuitive level before attempting the mathematical statement of the Efficient Market Hypothesis (EMH) in Appendix B. We have also occasionally referred to these notions in parenthetical remarks or footnotes to be more precise about a point in the text.

A-1. EXPECTATION

Suppose you engage in a game with someone in which you win one dollar from him if the flip of a coin results in a head, and you lose a dollar to him if the flip of the coin results in a tail. The coin, we assume, has a 50-50 chance of turning up heads. The outcome of the flip is a random event, so the payment (receipt) of money is a random variable. The expectation of this game is defined to be equal to the product of what you can win multiplied by the probability of winning, less the product of what you can lose multiplied by the probability of losing. In the example $\$1(\frac{1}{2}) - \$1(\frac{1}{2}) = \$0$.

This was an even or "fair" game. No one had an advantage. Whenever the game is a fair game the expectation will be zero. Note that you do not receive the expectation on any one play. On a single play you either win or lose one dollar. But on two plays you would *expect*, on the average, to win once and lose once, a net of zero over the two plays. In this sense the concept of an expectation is a long-run average notion. Indeed, we often refer to the expected return as the average or mean return.

For a second example, suppose the dollar bet is resolved by the roll of an honest die where you win on the numbers 1 through 4 inclusive. The expectation of this new game is $\$1(4/6) - \$1(2/6) = \$2/6 = \$0.33$. The positive expectation indicates the game is in your favor as far as the monetary amount is concerned.

Formally, we express the expectation using the letter E and place the variable (winnings above) in parentheses. Thus, if we let x_i be the amount won, for the second example, we have

$$\text{Expected Value} = \$1(4/6) + (-\$1)(2/6)$$
$$E(\tilde{X}) = x_1 \cdot p(x_1) + x_2 \cdot p(x_2)$$

$\tilde{X} \equiv$ the amount of money received. The tilde ($\sim$)
signifies that this amount is a random variable

where:

$x_1 \equiv x_{\text{win}} \equiv$ the amount to be won

$x_2 \equiv x_{\text{lose}} \equiv$ the amount to be lost

$p(x_1) \equiv p(x_{\text{win}}) \equiv$ the probability of winning

and $\quad p(x_2) \equiv p(x_{lose}) \equiv$ the probability of losing.

In the most general notational form, we write

$$E(\tilde{X}) = \sum_i x_i \cdot p(x_i). \tag{A1}$$

A-2. VARIANCE

We observed that in one play of either of the games described in the previous subsection the expected value would not be the result. Hence, in the second example, the expectation is $0.33. Yet on a single play the result is either a dollar won or a dollar lost. The variance is one measure of the dispersion of the actual returns about the mean or expected return. More precisely, it measures the average squared deviation of the actual returns around the expectation. Each possible deviation is weighted by its likelihood. For the second example, we have

$$\text{Variance} = (1-.33)^2 \, (4/6) + (-1-.33)^2 \, (2/6)$$
$$\text{Var } (\tilde{X}) = (.67)^2 \, (4/6) + (-1.33)^2 \, (2/6)$$
$$\sigma^2 \, (\tilde{X}) = 0.89.$$

The use of the variance as a measure of the dispersion of the returns implicitly assumes that the effect of variability is best captured by the square of the difference between a particular return and the expectation. Thus, a return that is twice as far removed from the expectation as some other return is four times as important in measuring the impact of the variability of the return.

Using general notation, the variance is written as

$$\sigma^2 \, (\tilde{X}) = E \, ([\tilde{X} - E(\tilde{X})]^2$$
$$= \sum_i [x_i - E(\tilde{X})]^2 \cdot p(x_i) \tag{A2}$$

The square root of the variance is the standard deviation and is denoted by the symbol $\sigma(\tilde{X})$.

The reader will note that we have considered only variables that take on measurable probabilities at discrete points. This is done on purpose, since only discrete variables are required to understand the material in this book. Formulas for continuous variables are similar to (A1) and (A2) except that: (1) an integration sign replaces the summation symbol and (2) the expression $f(x)dx$ replaces $p(x_i)$ to caution the reader that a probability density function, which is required for a continuous variable, is being used.

A-3. COVARIANCE

The prefix *co-* signifies together or joint. A covariance relates to two variables rather than just one. It measures how the two variables vary in a joint sense: Do they rise together, fall together, or move with no apparent joint relationship?

We can again use a simple gambling analogy to illustrate this concept. Suppose, based on the roll of a die, you receive from two other players (or, alternatively, make to two other players) the following dollar payments:

Event	Result of Die	Probability	Received from (Paid to) Player X	Received from (Paid to) Player Y
1	1 or 2	1/3	+$1	−$1
2	3 or 4	1/3	0	0
3	5 or 6	1/3	−$1	+$1

The minus sign indicates a payment made, the plus sign a payment received.

In this case the payments to players X and Y move opposite to one another. They vary inversely rather than directly. When the payment to one player is high, the payment to the other is low, and vice versa. The covariance is measured as the sum of several products. Each of these is the product of the differences of the payoffs from their own expectation for each variable under each event.

$$\text{Covariance} = [x_1 - E(\tilde{X})][y_1 - E(\tilde{Y})] \cdot p(x_1, y_1)$$
$$+ [x_2 - E(\tilde{X})][y_2 - E(\tilde{Y})] \cdot p(x_2, y_2)$$
$$+ [x_3 - E(\tilde{X})][y_3 - E(\tilde{Y})] \cdot p(x_3, y_3)$$
$$\text{Cov } (\tilde{X}, \tilde{Y}) = [1-0][-1-0] \cdot 1/3 + [0-0][0-0] \cdot 1/3$$
$$+ [-1-0][1-0] \cdot 1/3$$
$$\sigma(\tilde{X}, \tilde{Y}) = -1/3 + 0 - 1/3 = -2/3$$

The negative value reflects the inverse relationship.

The symbol $p(x_i y_i)$ stands for the joint probability that x and y take on the indicated values simultaneously. Thus, the probability that both payoffs are zero at the same time, $p(x = 0, y = 0) = p(x_2, y_2)$, is the probability the die shows a 3 or a 4. This occurs one-third of the time. Hence $p(x_2, y_2) = 1/3$.

In general terms, we may write the covariance as:

$$\sigma(\tilde{X}, \tilde{Y}) = E([\tilde{X} - E(\tilde{X})] \cdot [\tilde{Y} - E(\tilde{Y})]$$
$$= \sum_i [x_i - E(\tilde{X})] \cdot [y_i - E(\tilde{Y})] \cdot p(x_i, y_i). \tag{A3}$$

To illustrate the effect on the covariance when the variables move together, suppose the payoffs received from Y were $1 for a one or two on the die, 0 for a three or four, and −$1 for a five or six. The payoffs from X remain unchanged. Then

$$\sigma(\tilde{X}, \tilde{Y}) = [1-0][1-0] \cdot 1/3 + [0-0][0-0] \cdot 1/3 + [-1-0][-1-0] \cdot 1/3$$
$$= 2/3.$$

In this case the positive value reflects the direct relationship. When there is little or no relationship between the movement of two variables, the covariance is close to zero. This is illustrated by the following set of values:

x_i	y_i	$p(x_i, y_i)$
2	-1	1/4
2	$+1$	1/4
-2	-1	1/4
-2	$+1$	1/4

The expected values of both X and Y are zero using formula (A1). The covariance is given by:

$$\sigma(\tilde{X}, \tilde{Y}) = [2-0][-1-0] \cdot 1/4 + [2-0][1-0] \cdot 1/4 + [-2-0][-1-0] \cdot 1/4$$
$$+ [-2-0][1-0] \cdot 1/4$$
$$= -1/2 + 1/2 + 1/2 - 1/2$$
$$= 0.$$

The three cases we have discussed in regard to the covariance are illustrated in Figure A-1. The positive relationship $\sigma(\tilde{X}, \tilde{Y}) > 0$ is suggested by the solid line sloping upward to the right. The negative relationship $\sigma(\tilde{X}, \tilde{Y}) < 0$ is illustrated by the dashed line sloping downward

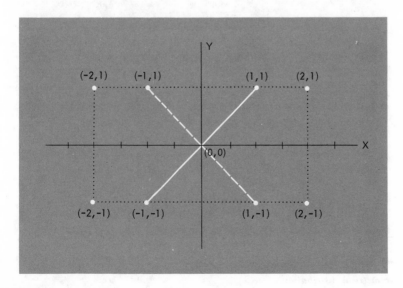

FIGURE A-1

Illustration of three separate types of covariance

to the right. The lack of a definite relationship is indicated by the dotted box-like figure involving the points (2,−1), (2,+1), (−2,−1) and (−2,+1).

In general, then, if two variables tend to move together, their covariance will be positive. If they tend to move inversely with one another, their covariance will be negative. And if such movements tend to cancel out, their covariance will be near zero.

A-4. SKEWNESS

A set of data can usually be described by a number of measures. One measure which describes the non-symmetrical characteristics of a set of data is called skewness. The histogram in Figure A-2 illustrates a symmetrical distribution while that in Figure A-3 illustrates a distribution that is skewed to the right.

There are several ways of measuring the skewness of the outcomes

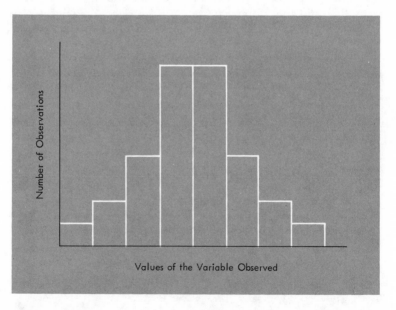

FIGURE A-2

A symmetrical distribution

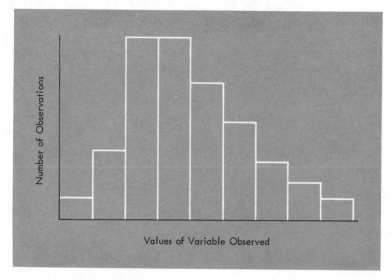

FIGURE A-3

Distribution skewed to the right

of a random variable. One simple measure is calculated using the formula:

$$\text{Skewness} = \frac{E([\tilde{X}-E(\tilde{X})]^3)}{[\sigma(\tilde{X})]^3}$$

A symmetrical distribution will have a zero skewness, while a distribution skewed to the right (left) will have a positive (negative) skewness measure. Calculation of the skewness for each of the gambles described in Section A-1 yields:

	Game 1	*Game 2*
Expectation, $E(\tilde{X})$	$0	$0.33
Standard Deviation, $\sigma(\tilde{X})$	1.0	0.943
Skewness	0	—0.70

APPENDIX B

A Mathematical Statement of the Efficient Market Hypothesis and Supporting Models

The purpose of this appendix is to present a concise mathematical representation of the various models that have found extensive use in the research into efficient markets. Reference to several of these models is made at various places in the text.

B-1. THE EXPECTED-RETURNS MODEL

The essence of the Efficient Market Hypothesis (EMH) is stated mathematically in the expected-returns model. The model, suggested by Fama [1970], is given by:

$$Z_{i,t+1} = r_{i,t+1} - E[\tilde{r}_{i,t+1} \mid \phi_t] \qquad (B1)$$

with

$$E[\tilde{Z}_{i,t+1} \mid \phi_t] = 0 \qquad (B2)$$

where $Z_{i,t+1}$ is the unexpected (or excess) return for security i in period $t+1$, the difference between the observed return, $r_{i,t+1}$, and the expected return based on the information set ϕ_t. The expected-return term obtains its value from some theory of expected returns beyond the expected-return model; for example, this value could be based on the Capital Asset Pricing Model (CAPM) [Sharpe 1964] to be described later in this appendix.

By defining information in different ways, Fama [1970] suggests three levels of market efficiency: the weak, the semi-strong, and the strong form. The weak form of the hypothesis states that equilibrium prices reflect fully any information contained in the sequence of historical prices. In its semi-strong form, the hypothesis is extended to incorporate all publicly available information and hence is of particular interest to accountants because financial statements are contained in the information set. The strong form adds inside information. This information specification is represented in the model by the ϕ_t term and, as the subscript denotes, is time specific.

The various empirical tests of the EMH described in Chapters 2, 3, and 4 have grown out of the implications that can be derived from the mathematical specifications given in equations (B1) and (B2).

B-2. THE CAPITAL ASSET PRICING MODEL

The EMH as expressed by the expected-returns model and summarized by equations (B1) and (B2) requires the use of expected returns in the expectation term of the first equation. Further, if an efficient market is a reasonably accurate hypothesis, then securities are (approximately) properly priced relative to each other. To specify appropriate relationships between individual stocks' expected returns in order to establish specific stock prices, we can use the Capital Asset Pricing Model (CAPM) developed by Sharpe [1964], Lintner [1965A], and Mossin [1966]. This model may be expressed mathematically as:

$$E(\tilde{r}_{it}) = r_{ft} + [E(\tilde{r}_{mt}) - r_{ft}] \frac{\sigma(\tilde{r}_{it}, \tilde{r}_{mt})}{\sigma^2(\tilde{r}_{mt})} \tag{B3}$$

where

$E(\tilde{r}_{it}) \equiv$ the expected return of security i in period t.

$r_{ft} \equiv$ the return on a riskless asset in period t.

$E(\tilde{r}_{mt}) \equiv$ the expected return on the market portfolio in period t.

$\sigma(\tilde{r}_{it}, \tilde{r}_{mt}) \equiv$ the covariance between $\tilde{r}_{it}$ and $\tilde{r}_{mt}$ (see Appendix A for a discussion of covariance)

$\sigma^2(\tilde{r}_{mt}) \equiv$ the variance of the return on the market portfolio.

This model embodies the following assumptions:

1. Investors are risk-averse, single period, expected-utility-of-terminal-wealth maximizers who select their holdings of securities on the basis of the mean and variance of the probability distribution of returns.
2. Investors can borrow or lend unlimited amounts at a common and exogenously determined riskless rate (r_{ft}).
3. Investors have homogeneous expectations; that is, they agree about the means, variances, and covariances of returns among all securities.
4. Perfect capital markets exist; that is, investors are price takers. There are no taxes or transactions costs, and all investors have equal and costless access to information.
5. The quantities of securities are fixed.

Thus the capital asset pricing model asserts that the only variable which determines the differences in expected returns is the risk coefficient given by

$$\lambda_i = \frac{\sigma(\tilde{r}_{it}, \tilde{r}_{mt})}{\sigma^2(\tilde{r}_{mt})} \tag{B4}$$

and that the relationship between this risk coefficient and expected return is linear. The risk coefficient is the ratio of the covariance between the particular securities return and the market, to the variance of the market. When the security's return and the market move together then $\sigma(\tilde{r}_{it}, \tilde{r}_{mt})$ will be positive. The closer the covariability, the larger the risk measure.

The CAPM is neutral concerning the process that generates security prices. However, some such assumption is generally necessary in order to estimate the expected-return series employed in tests of the efficient market using the expected-returns model. To provide for this need the market model developed by Markowitz [1952] and Sharpe [1963] has been extensively used.

The Market Model

The market model developed in conjunction with portfolio theory states that security returns are a linear function of a general market factor. The relationship can be written as:

$$\tilde{r}_{it} = a_i + \beta_i \tilde{R}_{mt} + \tilde{\mu}_{it} \tag{B5}$$

where

$E(\tilde{\mu}_{it}) = 0$.

$\sigma(\tilde{R}_{mt}, \tilde{\mu}_{it}) = 0$.

$\sigma(\tilde{\mu}_{it}, \tilde{\mu}_{jt}) = 0$.

$\tilde{r}_{it} \equiv$ return on security i in period t.

$\tilde{R}_{mt} \equiv$ general market factor in period t.

$\tilde{\mu}_{it} \equiv$ the stochastic portion of the individualistic factor representing the part of security i's return which is independent of $\tilde{R}_{mt}$.

$a_i, \beta_i \equiv$ intercept and slope respectively, of the linear relationship.

Basically, the model states that the stochastic portion of a security's return can be separated into a systematic component, represented by $\beta_i \tilde{R}_{mt}$, and an individualistic component, $\tilde{\mu}_{it}$.

The general market factor in equation (B5) is designed to reflect general market and economic conditions that are related to the returns on a particular security. This is a different notion than the return on the market portfolio in the CAPM given by $\tilde{r}_{mt}$. For this reason different symbols are used to represent these two similar but distinct concepts.

The only assumption needed for the market model is the first assumption of the CAPM: namely, that investors are risk-averse, single period, expected-utility-of-terminal-wealth maximizers who select their holdings of securities on the basis of the mean and variance of the distribution of returns.[1] In empirical research studies, estimates of a_i and β_i for each security are obtained from past data using ordinary least squares regression.

---

[1] The risk-averse assumption based on the mean-variance argument is consistent with maximizing the expected utility of terminal wealth only under severely restrictive conditions. Few decreasingly risk-averse utility functions can be integrated with the normal probability density function.

The market model hypothesizes a stochastic process that generates security returns. It is consistent with several alternate equilibrium pricing models of which the Lintner, Sharp, and Mossin models are only a few. Acceptance of the market model does not compel acceptance of the Lintner et al. CAPM or vice versa. However, the links between these two models through the expected-return model suggest the value to be obtained by connecting them.

The discussion of the two models and the assumptions behind them given here is intentionally brief. A more extensive coverage is available in Beaver [1972]. Also, a nontechnical discussion of beta (β_i) is given by Welles [1971].

B-3. THE ABNORMAL PERFORMANCE INDEX (API)

Accounting researchers have used the models discussed above to examine empirically the effects of accounting numbers. One of the more imaginative developments in this approach was the development of the Abnormal Performance Index (API) by Ball and Brown [1968] to study the association between unexpected changes in accounting earnings and unexpected changes in prices.

A form of the market model with coefficients based on a time series regression is used to form earnings expectations conditional on the observed *ex post* value of a market earnings factor. The residual, call it e_{it} for earnings residual, is the earnings forecast error assuming the model is an appropriate expression of expectations. The signs of the earnings forecast errors for the various securities are used to form portfolios. Simultaneously, the market model is also used to compute a price residual, the unexpected change in price μ_{it}, again conditional on the observed *ex post* market price. The unexpected price changes are aggregated (for the portfolios formed using the sign of the earnings forecast error) using the relationship

$$\text{API} = \frac{1}{N} \cdot \sum_i^N \prod_t^T (1 + \mu_{it}) - 1 \tag{B6}$$

$T \equiv$ number of time periods: $t = 1, 2, \ldots T$

$N \equiv$ number of securities: $i = 1, 2, \ldots, N$

$\mu_{it} \equiv$ individualistic component of r_{it} or, alternately, the forecast error.

The API traces out the value of a dollar invested in equal amounts in each security in the portfolio from time t up to time T. At time T the earnings number is assumed to be made public.

As Beaver [1972] notes, the API has an appealing intuitive interpretation. It represents one measure of the value of the information contained in the earnings number (actually the sign of the earnings forecast error) T months prior to the release of the earnings number. In this sense the API concept has some aspects of similarity to the notion of perfect information as the concept is used in decision theory. The analogy is not perfect, however, for the API is an *ex post* concept while the value of perfect information is an *ex ante* notion.

The API measures the return obtained from a specific and unusual investment strategy. The index assumes that information is obtained by the investor (in most studies) 12 months before it is public knowledge. The information received by the investor is a forecast of whether a firm's earnings will increase or decrease. The investor then adopts a long position (he buys) in the firm's stock if the earnings change forecast is positive or a short position if the change forecasted is negative. The API measures the return obtained from this strategy. In obtaining the value of the index, both the earnings expectation and the return obtained are adjusted for market change. Hence the earnings change forecasted is the change over and above that which would be due to the movement of earnings levels generally; it is the unexpected earnings change. Likewise it is the unexpected return, the security's return after allowing for the effect on the firm's stock price of the overall market movement, that is used to measure the abnormal performance. The investor is assumed to know the sign of the unexpected earnings change and the methodology determines whether this allows the investor to make an unexpected (abnormal) return.

The API implies a portfolio in which an equal dollar investment is made in each security at the start of the analysis and this investment is not altered over the period studied. An alternative formulation advanced by Fama et al. [1969] asumes a portfolio in which the investment in each security is adjusted through transactions so that an equal dollar investment for each security holds at the start of each period. This is a rebalancing approach. The Fama formulation is called the cumulative average residual.

The transactions implied by the Fama approach, an equal dollar investment in each security at the start of each period, make it less appealing than the simple buy-and-hold strategy implicit to the API. On the other hand the API also has limitations. First it assumes that the systematic risk of the portfolio is constant, i.e., in proportion to the initial weights reflected by $1/N$. But as the monthly weights change due to the buy-and-hold strategy so does the systematic risk. Second, the API involves a number of cross product terms due to the multiplicative nature of the formulation and may be dominated by these cross product terms when measured over many time periods. Ball [1972] has observed that the API is misleading over long periods if the monthly abnormal performance is either consistently positive or consistently negative. For example, the reinvestment of initial negative performance at a negative rate produces a positive return which is difficult to interpret. Third, the API uses only a limited, but important, portion of the data contained in financial reports. Recent studies can be found which use either the Ball and Brown or the Fama method depending on the merits of the two approaches as evaluated by the researcher.

References

ABER, J., "Multi-Index Linear Assessment Models of Security Return." Unpublished D. B. A. Dissertation, Harvard Graduate School of Business Administration, 1972.

ALEXANDER, S., "Price Movements in Speculative Markets: Trends or Random Walks," *Industrial Management Review* (May 1961), pp. 7-26.

ARCHIBALD, T., "Stock Market Reaction to the Depreciation Switch-Bank," *The Accounting Review* (January 1972), pp. 22-30.

ARDITTI, F., "Risk and the Required Return on Equity," *Journal of Finance* (March 1967), pp. 19-36.

———, "Another Look at Mutual Fund Performance," *Journal of Financial and Quantitative Analysis* (June 1971), pp. 909-912.

ARROW, K., *Social Choice and Individual Values.* 2nd edition. New York: Wiley, 1953.

———, and F. HAHN, *General Competitive Analysis.* San Francisco: Holden-Day, 1971.

BACHELIER, L., "Théorie de la Spéculation" (Paris: Gauthrei-Villars, 1900), translated version in Paul H. Cootner, *The Random Character of Stock Market Prices.* Cambridge, Massachusetts: The M.I.T. Press, 1964, pp. 17-78.

BALL, R., "Changes in Accounting Technique and Stock Prices," *Empirical Research in Accounting: Selected Studies 1972,* supplement to the *Journal of Accounting Research* (1972), pp. 1-38.

————, and P. BROWN, "An Empirical Evaluation of Accounting Income Numbers," *Journal of Accounting Research* (Autumn 1968), pp. 159-178.

————, and ————, "Portfolio Theory and Accounting," *Journal of Accounting Research* (Autumn 1969), pp. 300-323.

BASU, S., "Investment Performance and Price Ratios," Unpublished Ph.D. Dissertation, Cornell University, 1974.

BEAVER, W., "The Information Content of Annual Earnings Announcements," *Empirical Research in Accounting: Selected Studies 1968,* supplement to the *Journal of Accounting Research* (1968), pp. 67-92.

————, "The Time Series Behavior of Earnings," *Empirical Research in Accounting: Selected Studies 1970,* supplement to the *Journal of Accounting Research* (1970), pp. 62-107.

————, "The Behavior of Security Prices and Its Implications for Accounting Research (Methods)," *Supplement to The Accounting Review* (1972), pp. 407-437.

————, "What Should be the Objectives of the FASB?" *Journal of Accountancy* (August 1973), pp. 49-56.

————, "Implications of Security Price Research for Accounting: A Reply to Bierman," *The Accounting Review* (July 1974), pp. 563-571.

————, and J. DEMSKI, "The Nature of Financial Accounting Objectives," Stanford Working Paper, 1974.

————, and R. DUKES, "Interperiod Tax Allocation, Earnings Expectations, and the Behavior of Security Prices," *The Accounting Review* (April 1972), pp. 320-332.

————, and R. DUKES, "Interperiod Tax Allocation and Delta-Depreciation Methods: Some Empirical Results," *The Accounting Review* (July 1973), pp. 549-559.

————, T. P. KETTLER, and M. SCHOLES, "The Association Between Market Determined and Accounting Determined Risk Measures," *The Accounting Review* (October 1970), pp. 654-682.

————, and J. Manegold, "The Association Between Market-Determined and Accounting-Determined Measures of Systematic Risk: Some Further Evidence," Stanford Working Paper, August-September 1973.

BENSTON, G., "Published Corporate Accounting Data and Stock Prices," *Empirical Research in Accounting: Selected Studies 1967,* supplement to the *Journal of Accounting Research* (1967), pp. 1-54.

———, "Required Disclosure and the Stock Market: An Evaluation of the Securities Exchange Act of 1934," *American Economic Review* (March 1973) pp. 132-155.

BIERMAN, H., "The Implications of Efficient Markets and the Capital Asset Pricing Model to Accounting," *The Accounting Review* (July 1974), pp. 557-562.

BLACK, F., "Capital Market Equilibrium with Restricted Borrowing," *Journal of Business* (July 1972), pp. 444-455.

———, M. Jensen, and M. Scholes, "The Capital Asset Pricing Model: Some Empirical Tests," in Jensen (ed.), *Studies in the Theory of Capital Markets*. New York: Praeger, 1972.

———, and M. SCHOLES, "The Valuation of Option Contracts and a Test of Market Efficiency," *Journal of Finance* (May 1972), pp. 399-417.

———, and ———, "The Pricing of Options and Corporate Liabilities," *Journal of Political Economy* (May-June 1973), pp. 637-654.

BLUME, M., "Portfolio Theory: A Step Toward Its Practical Application," *Journal of Business* (April 1970), pp. 152-173.

———, "On the Assessment of Risk," *Journal of Finance* (March 1971), pp. 1-10.

———, and I. FRIEND, "A New Look at the Capital Asset Pricing Model," *Journal of Finance* (March 1973), pp. 19-33.

BREEN, W., "Low Price-Earnings Ratios and Industry Relatives," *Financial Analysts Journal* (July-August 1968), pp. 125-127.

———, and J. SAVAGE, "Portfolio Distribution and Tests of Security Selection Models," *Journal of Finance* (December 1968), pp. 805-819.

BRENNAN, M., "An Approach to the Valuations of Uncertain Income Streams," *Journal of Finance* (June 1973), pp. 661-674.

BRENNER, M., "A Note on Risk, Return and Equilibrium: Empirical Tests," Cornell Working Paper, April 1974A.

———, "The Sensitivity of the Efficient Market Hypothesis to Alternate Specifications of the Market Model." Unpublished Ph.D. Dissertation, Cornell University, 1974B.

———, and S. SMIDT, "Predicting Changes in Systematic Risk: Theory and Evidence," Revised Working Paper, Cornell University, Spring 1974.

BRILOFF, A., *Unaccountable Accounting*. New York: Harper & Row, 1972.

BROWN, P., and J. KENNELLY, "The Informational Content of Quarterly Earnings: An Extension and Some Further Evidence," *Journal of Business* (July 1972), pp. 403-415.

CHENG, P., and M. Deets, "Portfolio Returns and the Random Walk Theory," *Journal of Finance* (March 1971), pp. 1-10.

———, and ———, "Systematic Risk and the Horizon Problem," *Journal of Financial and Quantitative Analysis* (March 1973), pp. 299-316.

COLLINS, D., "SEC Product-line Reporting and Market Efficiency," *Journal of Financial Economics*, forthcoming.

COMISKEY, E., "Market Response to Changes in Depreciation Accounting," *The Accounting Review* (April 1971), pp. 279-285.

COOTNER, P., "Stock Prices: Random vs. Systematic Changes," *Industrial Management Review* (Spring 1972), pp. 22-45.

COWLES, A., and H. JONES, "Some A Posteriori Probabilities in Stock Market Action," *Econometrica* (July 1937), pp. 280-294.

CROUCH, R., "The Volume of Transactions and Price Changes on the New York Stock Exchange," *Financial Analysts Journal* (July-August 1970), pp. 104-109.

DEMSKI, J., "The General Impossibility of Normative Accounting Standards," *The Accounting Review* (October 1973), pp. 718-723.

―――, "Choice Among Financial Reporting Alternatives," *The Accounting Review* (April 1974), pp. 221-232.

DOUGLAS, G., "Risk in the Equity Markets: An Empirical Appraisal of Market Efficiency," *Yale Economic Essays* (Spring 1969), pp. 3-45.

DOWNES, D., and T. DYCKMAN, "A Critical Look at the Efficient Market Empirical Research Literature as it Relates to Accounting Information," *The Accounting Review* (April 1973), pp. 300-317.

DYCKMAN, T., "Decision Models and Accounting Measurement." Monograph published by the Stanford University Press in the Price Waterhouse Lecture Series, Fall 1971.

EVANS, J., and S. ARCHER, "Diversification and the Reduction of Dispersion: An Empirical Analysis," *Journal of Finance* (December 1968), pp. 761-767.

FAMA, E., "The Behavior of Stock Market Prices," *Journal of Business* (January 1965A), pp. 34-105.

―――, "Tomorrow on the New York Stock Exchange," *Journal of Business* (July 1965B), pp. 285-299.

―――, "Efficient Capital Markets: A Review of Theory and Empirical Work," *Journal of Finance* (May 1970), pp. 383-417.

―――, and M. BLUME, "Filter Rules and Stock Market Trading," *Journal of Business, Security Prices: A Supplement* (January 1966), pp. 226-241.

―――, L. FISHER, M. JENSEN, and R. ROLL, "The Adjustment of Stock Prices to New Information," *International Economic Review* (February 1969), pp. 1-21.

―――, and A. LAFFER, "Information and Capital Markets," *Journal of Business* (July 1971), pp. 289-298.

―――, and J. MACBETH, "Risk, Return and Equilibrium: Empirical Tests," *Journal of Political Economy* (May-June 1973), pp. 607-636.

FOSTER, G., "Stock Market Reaction to Estimates of Earnings Per Share by Company Officials," *Journal of Accounting Research* (Spring 1973), pp. 25-37.

FRIEND, I., and M. BLUME, "Measurement of Portfolio Performance Under Uncertainty," *American Economic Review* (September 1970), pp. 561-575.

————, ————, and J. CROCKETT, *Mutual Funds and Other Institutional Investors, A New Perspective.* A 20th Century Fund Study, New York: McGraw-Hill Book Co., 1970.

————, F. BROWN, E. HERMAN, and D. VICKERS, *A Study of Mutual Funds.* Prepared for the Securities and Exchange Commission by the Securities Research Unit, Wharton School of Finance and Commerce, University of Pennsylvania. Washington, D.C.: U.S. Government Printing Office, 1962.

GOLDMAN, M., "A Note on the Cheng and Deets Tests of the Random Walk Theory," *Journal of Finance,* forthcoming.

GONEDES, N., "The Significance of Selected Accounting Procedures: A Statistical Test," *Empirical Research in Accounting: Selected Studies 1969,* supplement to the *Journal of Accounting Research* (1969), pp. 90-113.

————, "Efficient Capital Markets and External Accounting," *The Accounting Review* (January 1972), pp. 11-21.

————, "Evidence on the Information Content of Accounting Messages: Accounting-Based and Market-Based Estimates of Systematic Risk," *Journal of Financial and Quantitative Analysis* (June 1973), pp. 407-444.

————, "Evidence on the Information Content of Accounting Messages: Accounting-Based and Market-Based Estimates of Systematic Risk," *Journal of Financial and Quantitative Analysis* (June 1973), pp. 407-444.

————, Capital Market Equilibrium and Annual Accounting Numbers: Empirical Evidence," *Journal of Accounting Research* (Spring 1974), forthcoming.

————, and N. DOPUCH, "Capital Market Equilibrium, Information-Production and Selecting Accounting Techniques: Theoretical Framework and Review of Empirical Work," presented at the Robert M. Trueblood Memorial Accounting Conference on Financial Accounting, University of Chicago, May 1974.

GRANGER, C., and O. MORGENSTERN, "Spectral Analysis of New York Stock Market Prices," *Kyklos* (1963), pp. 1-27.

————, and ————, *Predictability of Stock Market Prices.* New York: D. C. Heath & Co., 1970.

GRIER, P., and P. ALBIN, "Nonrandom Price Changes in Association with Trading in Large Blocks," *Journal of Business* (July 1973), pp. 425-433.

HAGERMAN, R., and R. RICHMOND, "Random Walks, Martingales and the OTC," *Journal of Finance* (September 1973), pp. 897-909.

HAMADA, R., "Portfolio Analysis, Market Equilibrium and Corporation Finance," *Journal of Finance* (March 1969), pp. 13-32.

HIRSHLEIFER, J., "The Private and Social Value of Information and the Reward for Intensive Activity," *American Economic Review* (September 1971), pp. 561-574.

HOMA, K., and D. JAFFEE, "The Supply of Money and Common Stock Prices," *Journal of Finance* (December 1971), pp. 1045-1066.

JACOB, N., "The Measurement of Systematic Risk for Securities and Portfolios: Some Empirical Results," *Journal of Financial and Quantitative Analysis* (March 1971), pp. 815-833.

————, "Comment: Systematic Risk and the Horizon Problem," *Journal of Financial and Quantitative Analysis* (March 1973), pp. 351-416.

JAFFE, J., "Special Information and Insider Trading," *Journal of Business* (July 1974), pp. 410-428.

JENSEN, M., "Random Walks: Reality or Myth—Comment," *Financial Analysts Journal* (November-December 1967), pp. 77-85.

————, "The Performance of Mutual Funds in the Period 1945-1964," *Journal of Finance* (May 1968), pp. 389-416.

————, "Risk, the Pricing of Capital Assets, and the Evaluation of Investment Portfolios," *Journal of Business* (April 1969), pp. 167-247.

————, "The Foundations and Current State of Capital Market Theory," in Jensen (ed.), *Studies in the Theory of Capital Markets.* New York: Praeger, 1972.

————, and G. BENNINGTON, "Random Walks and Technical Theories: Some Additional Evidence," *Journal of Finance* (May 1970), pp. 469-482.

JONES, C., "Earnings Trends and Investment Selection," *Financial Analysts Journal* (March-April 1973), pp. 79-83.

————, and R. LITZENBERGER, "Quarterly Earnings Reports and Intermediate Stock Price Trends," *Journal of Finance* (March 1970), pp. 143-148.

JORDAN, R., "An Empirical Investigation of the Adjustment of Stock Prices to New Quarterly Earnings Information," *Journal of Financial and Quantitative Analysis* (September 1973), pp. 609-620.

KAPLAN, R. and R. ROLL, "Investor Evaluation of Accounting Information: Some Empirical Evidence," *Journal of Business* (April 1972), pp. 225-257.

KENDALL, R., "The Analysis of Economic Time Series, Part I: Prices," *Journal of the Royal Statistical Society,* Vol. 96, Part 1 (1953), pp. 11-25.

KIGER, J., "An Empirical Investigation of NYSE Volume and Price Reactions to the Announcement of Quarterly Earnings," *Journal of Accounting Research* (Spring 1972), pp. 113-128.

KING, B., "Market and Industry Factors in Stock Price Behavior," *Journal of Business* (January 1966), pp. 139-190.

KRAUS, A., and R. LITZENBERGER, "Skewness Preference and the Valuation of Risk Assets," Stanford Working Paper, December 1972.

————, and H. STOLL, "Price Impacts of Block Trading on the New York Stock Exchange," *Journal of Finance* (June 1972), pp. 569-588.

LEROY, S., "Risk Aversion and the Martingale Property of Stock Prices," *International Economic Review* (June 1973), pp. 436-446.

LEVY, H., "Portfolio Performance and the Investment Horizon," *Management Science* (August 1972), pp. B. 645-653.

LEVY, R., "Random Walks: Reality or Myth," *Financial Analysts Journal* (November-December 1967), pp. 69-76.

————, "On the Short-Term Stationarity of Beta Coefficients," *Financial Analysts Journal* (November-December 1971), pp. 55-62.

LINTNER, J., "The Valuation of Risky Assets and the Selection of Risky Investments in Stock Portfolios and Capital Budgets," *Review of Economics and Statistics* (February 1965A), pp. 13-37.

————, "Security Prices, Risk and Maximal Gains from Diversification," *Journal of Finance* (December 1965B), pp. 587-616.

————, "The Aggregation of Investors' Diverse Judgments and Preferences in Purely Competitive Security Markets," *Journal of Financial and Quantitative Analysis* (December 1969), pp. 347-400.

LOGUE, D., and L. MERVILLE, "Financial Policy and Market Expectations," *Financial Management* (Summer 1972), pp. 37-44.

LORIE, J., and M. HAMILTON, *The Stock Market: Theories and Evidence*. Homewood, Illinois: Richard D. Irwin, Inc., 1973.

————, and V. NIEDERHOFFER, "Predictive and Statistical Properties of Insider Trading," *Journal of Law and Economics* (April 1968), pp. 35-53.

MAGEE, R., "The Market Association of Accounting Earnings Numbers: Further Evidence," Unpublished Ph.D. Dissertation, Cornell University, 1974.

MALKIEL, B., and J. CRAGG, "Expectations and the Structure of Share Prices," *American Economic Review* (September 1970), pp. 601-617.

————, and R. QUANDT, "The Supply of Money and Common Stock Prices, A Comment," *Journal of Finance* (September 1972), pp. 921-926.

MARKOWITZ, H., "Portfolio Selection," *Journal of Finance* (March 1952), pp. 77-91.

MAY, R., "The Influence of Quarterly Earnings Announcements on Investor Decisions as Reflected in Common Stock Price Changes," *Empirical Research in Accounting: Selected Studies 1971*, supplement to the *Journal of Accounting Research* (1971), pp. 119-163.

————, and G. SUNDEM, "Cost of Information and Security Prices: Market Association Tests for Accounting Policy Decisions," *The Accounting Review* (January 1973), pp. 80-94.

MEYERS, S., "The Stationarity Problem in the Use of the Market Model of

Security Price Behavior," *The Accounting Review* (April 1973), pp. 318-322.

McKIBBEN, W., "Econometric Forecasting of Common Stock Individual Returns: A New Methodology Using Fundamental Operating Data," *Journal of Finance* (May 1972), pp. 371-380.

McWILLIAMS, J., "Prices, Earnings and P.E. Ratios," *Financial Analysts Journal* (May-June 1966), pp. 137-142.

MILLER, M., and M. SCHOLES, "Rates of Return in Relation to Risk: A Reexamination of Some Recent Findings," in Jensen (ed.), *Studies in the Theory of Capital Markets*. New York: Praeger, 1972.

MILLER, P., and E. WIDMANN, "Price Performance Outlook for High and Low P/E Stocks," *1966 Stock and Bond Issue, Commercial and Financial Chronicle* (29 September, 1966), pp. 26-28.

MLYNARCZYK, F., "An Empirical Study of Accounting Methods and Stock Prices," *Empirical Research in Accounting: Selected Studies 1969,* supplement to the *Journal of Accounting Research* (1969), pp. 63-81.

MOORE, A., "Some Characteristics of Changes in Common Stock Prices," in Paul H. Cootner, *The Random Character of Stock Market Prices*. Cambridge, Massachusetts: The M.I.T. Press, 1964, pp. 139-161.

MOSSIN, J., "Equilibrium in a Capital Asset Market," *Econometrica* (October 1966), pp. 768-783.

NICHOLSON, F., "Price Ratios in Relation to Investment Results," *Financial Analysts Journal* (January-February 1968), pp. 105-109.

NIEDERHOFFER, V., and M. OSBORNE, "Market Making and Reversal on the New York Stock Exchange," *Journal of the American Statistical Association* (December 1966), pp. 897-916.

O'DONNELL, JOHN L., "Relationships Between Reported Earnings and Stock Prices in the Electric Utility Industry," *The Accounting Review* (January 1965), pp. 135-143.

————, "Further Observations on Reported Earnings and Stock Prices," *The Accounting Review* (July 1968), pp. 549-553.

OSBORNE, M., "Brownian Motion in the Stock Market," *Operations Research* (March-April 1959), pp. 145-173.

————, "Periodic Structure in the Brownian Motion of Stock Prices," *Operations Research* (May-June 1962), pp. 345-379.

PATZ, DENNIS, and J. BOATSMAN, "Accounting Principle Formulation in an Efficient Markets Environment," *Journal of Accounting Research* (Autumn 1972), pp. 392-403.

PETTIT, R., "Dividend Announcements, Security Performances, and Capital Market Efficiency," *Journal of Finance* (December 1972), pp. 993-1007.

————, and R. Westerfield, "A Model of Market Risk," *Journal of Financial and Quantitative Analysis* (March 1972), pp. 1649-1668.

PHILIPPATOS, G., and D. NAWROCKI, "The Information Inaccuracy of Stock Market Forecasts: Some New Evidence of Dependence on the New York Stock Exchange," *Journal of Financial and Quantitative Analysis* (June 1973), pp. 445-58.

POGUE, G., and B. SOLNIK, "The Market Model Applied to European Common Stocks: Some Empirical Results," *Journal of Financial and Quantitative Analysis* (December 1974), pp. 917-944.

PRATT, S., and C. DE VERE, "Relationships Between Insider Trading and Rates of Return for NYSE Common Stocks, 1960-1966," paper presented at the Seminar on the Analysis of Security Prices, University of Chicago, May 1968.

REBACK, R., "Nonrandom Price Changes in Association with Trading in Large Blocks: A Comment," *Journal of Business* (October 1974), pp. 564-565.

ROBERTS, H., "Stock Market 'Patterns' and Financial Analysis: Methodological Suggestions," *Journal of Finance* (March 1959), pp. 1-10.

ROLL, R., *The Behavior of Interest Rates: An Application of the Efficient Market Model to U.S. Treasury Bills.* New York: Basic Books, 1970.

ROSENBERG, B., and M. HOUGLET, "Error Rates in CRSP and COMPUSTAT Data Bases and Their Implications," *Journal of Finance* (September 1974), pp. 1303-1310.

————, and W. MCKIBBEN, "The Prediction of Systematic and Specific Risk in Common Stocks," *Journal of Financial and Quantitative Analysis* (March 1973), pp. 317-333.

RUBENSTEIN, M., "Securities Market Efficiency in an Arrow-Debreu Economy," Working Paper: Research Program in Finance No. 14, University of California at Berkeley, October 1973, forthcoming in *American Economic Review.*

SAMUELSON, P., "Proof That Properly Anticipated Prices Fluctuate Randomly," *Industrial Management Review* (Spring 1965), pp. 41-49.

SCHOLES, M., "The Market for Securities: Substitution versus Price Pressure and the Effects of Information on Share Prices," *Journal of Business* (April 1972), pp. 179-211.

SHARPE, W., "A Simplified Model for Portfolio Analysis," *Management Science* (January 1963), pp. 277-293.

————, "Capital Asset Prices: A Theory of Market Equilibrium Under Conditions of Risk," *Journal of Finance* (September 1964), pp. 425-442.

————, "Mutual Fund Performance," *Journal of Business, Security Prices: A Supplement* (January 1966), pp. 119-138.

————, *Portfolio Theory and Capital Markets,* New York: McGraw-Hill Book Co., 1970.

————, and G. COOPER, "Risk-Return Classes of New York Stock Exchange

Common Stocks, 1931-1967," *Financial Analysts Journal* (March-April 1972), pp. 46-54.

SMIDT, S., "A New Look at the Random-Walk Hypothesis," *Journal of Financial and Quantitative Analysis* (September 1968), pp. 235-261.

STERLING, ROBERT, "On Theory Construction and Verification," *The Accounting Review* (July 1970), pp. 444-57.

STIGLITZ, J., "Some Aspects of the Pure Theory of Corporate Finance: Bankruptcies and Take-Overs," *The Bell Journal of Economics and Management Science* (Autumn 1972), pp. 458-481.

STONE, B., "Capital Market Equilibrium with Restricted Borrowing: Some Clarifying Comments," Cornell Working Paper, Fall 1972.

————, "Asset Pricing in the Absence of a Riskless Asset—A Clarification of the Zero-Beta Concept," Cornell Working Paper, November 1973.

————, "Warrent Betas," Cornell Working Paper, 1974, forthcoming *Journal of Finance*.

SUNDER, S., "Relationship Between Accounting Changes and Stock Prices: Problems of Measurement and Some Empirical Evidence," *Empirical Research in Accounting: Selected Studies 1973*, supplement to *Journal of Accounting Research*, forthcoming.

WAGNER, W., and S. LAU, "The Effect of Diversification on Risk," *Financial Analysts Journal* (November-December 1971), pp. 48-53.

WATTS, R., "The Information Content of Dividends," *Journal of Business* (April 1973), pp. 191-211.

WAUD, R., "Public Interpretation of Federal Reserve Discount Rate Changes: Evidence on the Announcement Effect," *Econometrica* (March 1970), pp. 231-250.

WELLES, C., "The Beta Revolution: Learning to Live with Risk," *Institutional Investor* (September 1971), pp. 21-64.

WEST, R., and S. TINIC, "Portfolio Returns and the Random-Walk Theory: A Comment," *Journal of Finance* (June 1973), pp. 733-741.

WILLIAMSON, J., "Measuring Mutual Fund Performance," *Financial Analysts Journal* (November-December 1972), pp. 78-84.

WORKING, H., "A Random Difference Series for Use in the Analysis of Time Series," *Journal of the American Statistical Association* (March 1934), pp. 11-24.

YING, C., "Stock Market Prices and Volume of Sales," *Econometrica* (July 1966), pp. 676-685.

ZWEIG, M., "An Investor Expectations Stock Price Predictive Model Using Closed-End Fund Premiums," *Journal of Finance* (March 1973), pp. 67-78.

Index

PRENTICE-HALL
CONTEMPORARY TOPICS IN ACCOUNTING SERIES

Alfred Rappaport, Series Editor

The Prentice-Hall Contemporary Topics in Account-
ing Series discusses significant recent developments
in accounting through brief self-contained studies.
These independent studies provide the reader with
up-to-date coverage of key topics that deal with chang-
ing business methods. The series offers a succinct
overview of developments in research and practice in
areas of special interest and its authoritative analyses
of controversial problems will stimulate independent
and creative thinking.

The books that form this series:

PRENTICE-HALL, INC., Englewood Cliffs, New Jersey

0-13-246967-